OLD MOORE'S

HOROSCOPE AND ASTRAL DIARY

PISCES

OLD MOORE'S

HOROSCOPE AND ASTRAL DIARY

PISCES

foulsham
LONDON • NEW YORK • TORONTO • SYDNEY

foulsham

The Old Barrel Store, Drayman's Lane, Marlow, Bucks SL7 2FF

Foulsham books can be found in all good bookshops and direct from
www.foulsham.com

ISBN: 978-0-572-04497-8

Copyright © 2014 W. Foulsham & Co. Ltd

A CIP record for this book is available from the British Library

Typeset in Great Britain by Chris Brewer Origination, Christchurch

CONTENTS

INTRODUCTION

Astrology has been a part of life for centuries now, and no matter how technological our lives become, it seems that it never diminishes in popularity. For thousands of years people have been gazing up at the star-clad heavens and seeing their own activities and proclivities reflected in the movement of those little points of light. Across centuries countless hours have been spent studying the way our natures, activities and decisions seem to be paralleled by their predictable movements. Old Moore, a time-served veteran in astrological research, continues to monitor the zodiac and has produced the Astral Diary for 2015, tailor-made to your own astrological makeup.

Old Moore's Astral Diary is unique in its ability to get the heart of your nature and to offer you the sort of advice that might come from a trusted friend. It enables you to see in a day-by-day sense exactly how the planets are working for you. The diary section advises how you can get the best from upcoming situations and allows you to plan ahead successfully. There's also room on each daily entry to record your own observations or appointments.

While other popular astrology books merely deal with your astrological 'Sun sign', the Astral Diaries go much further. Every person on the planet is unique and Old Moore allows you to access your individuality in a number of ways. The front section gives you the chance to work out the placement of the Moon at the time of your birth and to see how its position has set an important seal on your overall nature. Perhaps most important of all, you can use the Astral Diary to discover your Rising Sign. This is the zodiac sign that was appearing over the Eastern horizon at the time of your birth and is just as important to you as an individual as is your Sun sign.

It is the synthesis of many different astrological possibilities that makes you what you are and with the Astral Diaries you can learn so much. How do you react to love and romance? Through the unique Venus tables and the readings that follow them, you can learn where the planet Venus was at the time of your birth. It is even possible to register when little Mercury is 'retrograde', which means that it appears to be moving backwards in space when viewed from the Earth. Mercury rules communication, so be prepared to deal with a few setbacks in this area when you see the sign ☿. The Astral Diary will be an interest and a support throughout the whole year ahead.

Old Moore extends his customary greeting to all people of the Earth and offers his age-old wishes for a happy and prosperous period ahead.

THE ESSENCE OF PISCES

Exploring the Personality of
Pisces the Fishes

(20TH FEBRUARY – 20TH MARCH)

What's in a sign?

Pisceans are fascinating people – everyone you come across is likely to admit that fact. By nature you are kind, loving, trustful and inclined to work very hard on behalf of the people you love – and perhaps even those you don't like very much. Your nature is sympathetic and you will do anything you can to improve the lot of those you consider to be worse off than yourself. There is a very forgiving side to your temperament and also a strong artistic flair that can find an outlet in any one of a dozen different ways.

It's true you are difficult to know, and there is a very important reason for this. Your nature goes deep, so deep in fact that someone would have to live with you for a lifetime to plumb even a part of its fathomless depths. What the world sees is only ever a small part of the total magic of this most compulsive and fascinating zodiac sign. Much of your latent power and natural magic is constantly kept bottled up, because it is never your desire to manipulate those around you. Rather, you tend to wait in the shadows until opportunities to come into your own present themselves.

In love you are ardent and sincere, though sometimes inclined to choose a partner too readily and too early. There's a dreamy quality to your nature that makes you easy to adore, but which can also cause difficulties if the practical necessities of life take a very definite second place.

The chances are that you love music and picturesque scenery, and you may also exhibit a definite fondness for animals. You prefer to live in the country rather than in the middle of a noisy and smelly town, and tend to keep a reasonably well-ordered household. Your family can easily become your life and you always need a focus for your energies. You are not at all good at feathering your own nest, unless you know that someone else is also going to benefit on the way. A little more selfishness probably would not go amiss on occasions because you are often far too willing to put yourself out wholesale for people who don't respect your sacrifices. Pisceans can be full of raging passions and are some of the most misunderstood people to be found anywhere within the great circle of the zodiac.

Pisces resources

It is the very essence of your zodiac sign that you are probably sitting there and saying to yourself 'Resources? I have no resources'. Of course you are wrong, though it has to be admitted that a glaring self-confidence isn't likely to be listed amongst them. You are, however, a very deep thinker, and this can turn out to be a great advantage and a useful tool when it comes to getting on in life. Because your natural intuition is so strong (some people would call you psychic), you are rarely fooled by the glib words of others. Your own natural tendency to tell the truth can be a distinct advantage and a great help to you when it comes to getting on in life from a practical and financial viewpoint.

Whilst many of the signs of the zodiac tend to respond to life in an impulsive way, you are more likely to weigh up the pros and cons of any given situation very carefully. This means that when you do take action you can achieve much more success – as well as saving a good deal of energy on the way. People tend to confide in you automatically, so you are definitely at an advantage when it comes to knowing what makes your family and friends tick. At work you can labour quietly and confidently, either on your own or in the company of others. Some people would assert that Pisceans are model employees because you really do not know how to give anything less than your best.

Never underestimate the power of your instincts. Under most circumstances you are aware of the possible outcome of any given situation and should react as your inner mind dictates. Following this course inevitably puts you ahead of the game and explains why so quiet a sign can promote so many winners in life. Not that you are particularly competitive. It's much more important for you to be part of a winning team than to be out there collecting the glory for yourself.

You are dependable, kind, loving and peerless in your defence of those you take to. All of these are incredible resources when used in the correct way. Perhaps most important of all is your ability to get others on your side. In this you cannot be matched.

Beneath the surface

Everyone instinctively knows that there is something very important going on beneath the surface of the Piscean mind, though working out exactly what it might be is a different kettle of fish altogether. The fact is that you are very secretive about yourself and tend to give very little away. There are occasions when this tendency can be a saving grace, but others where it is definitely a great disadvantage. What isn't hard to see is your natural sympathy and your desire to help those in trouble. There's no end gain here, it's simply the way you are. Your inspiration to do anything is rarely rooted in what your own prize is likely to be. In your soul you are poetical, deeply romantic and inextricably tied to the forces and cycles of the world that brought you to birth.

Despite your capacity for single-minded concentration in some matters, you are often subject to mental confusion. Rational considerations often take second place to intuitive foresight and even inspiration. Making leaps in logic isn't at all unusual for you and forms part of the way you judge the world and deal with it.

If you really want to get on in life, and to gain the most you can from your interactions with others, you need to be very truthful in your approach. Somehow or other that means finding out what is really going on in your mind and explaining it to those around you. This is never going to be an easy process, partly because of your naturally secretive ways. Actually some astrologers overplay the tendency of Pisces to keep its secrets. A great deal of the time you simply don't think you have anything to say that would interest others and you always lack confidence in your own judgements. This is a shame because you rarely proceed without thinking carefully and don't often make glaring mistakes.

Many Pisceans develop an ingrained tendency to believe themselves inadequate in some way. Once again this is something you should fight against. Knowing others better, and allowing them to get to know you, might cause you to feel less quirky or strange. Whether you realise it or not you have a natural magnetism that draws others towards you. Try to spend rather less time thinking – though without losing that Piscean ability to meditate which is central to your well-being. If you allow the fascinating world of the Piscean mind to be shared by the people you come to trust, you should become more understandable to people who really want to like you even more.

Making the best of yourself

It must be remembered that the zodiac sign of Pisces represents two Fishes, tethered by a cord but constantly trying to break away from each other. This says a great deal about the basic Piscean nature. The inward, contemplative side of your personality is often at odds with the more gregarious and chatty qualities you also possess. Learning about this duality of nature can go at least part of the way towards dealing with it.

Although you often exhibit a distinct lack of self-confidence in your dealings with the world at large, you are, at heart, quite adept, flexible and able to cope under almost any circumstance. All that is really required in order to have a positive influence on life and to be successful is for you to realise what you are capable of achieving. Alas this isn't quite as easy as it might appear, because the introspective depths of your nature make you think too much and cause you to avoid the very actions that would get you noticed more. This can be something of a dilemma for Pisces, though it is certainly not insurmountable.

Never be afraid to allow your sensitivity to show. It is one of your greatest assets and it is part of the reason why other people love you so much – far more, in fact, than you probably realise. Your natural warmth, grace and charm are certain to turn heads on those occasions when you can't avoid being watched. The creative qualities that you possess make it possible for you to manufacture harmonious surroundings, both for yourself and for your family, who are very important to you. At the same time you recognise the practical in life and don't mind getting your hands dirty, especially when it comes to helping someone else out of a mess.

One of the best ruses Pisceans can use in order to get over the innate shyness that often attends the sign is to put on an act. Pisceans are very good natural actors and can easily assume the role of another individual. So, in your dealings with the world at large, manufacture a more confident individual, though without leaving out all the wonderful things that make you what you are now. Play this part for all you are worth and you will then truly be making the best of yourself.

The impressions you give

There is absolutely no doubt that you are more popular, admired and even fancied than you could ever believe. Such is the natural modesty of your zodiac sign that you invariably fail to pick up on those little messages coming across from other people that say 'I think you are wonderful'. If we don't believe in ourselves it's difficult for us to accept that others think we are worth their consideration. Failing to realise your worth to the world at large is likely to be your greatest fault and needs to be corrected.

In a way it doesn't matter, when seen from the perspective of others. What they observe is a warm-hearted individual. Your magnetic personality is always on display, whether you intend it to be or not, which is another reason why you tend to attract far more attention than you would sometimes elicit. Most Pisceans are quite sexy, another quality that is bound to come across to the people you meet, at least some of whom would be willing to jump through hoops if you were to command it.

In short, what you show, and what you think you are, could be two entirely different things. If you don't believe this to be the case you need to carry out a straw poll amongst some of the people you know. Ask them to write down all your qualities as they see them. The result will almost certainly surprise you and demonstrate that you are far more capable, and loveable, than you believe yourself to be. Armed with this knowledge you can walk forward in life with more confidence and feel as content inside as you appear to be when viewed by the world at large.

People rely heavily on you. That much at least you will have noticed in a day-to-day sense. They do so because they know how well you deal with almost any situation. Even in a crisis you show your true colours and that's part of the reason why so many Piscean people find themselves involved in the medical profession. You are viewed as being stronger than you believe yourself to be, which is why everyone tends to be so surprised when they discover that you are vulnerable and inclined to worry.

The way forward

You have a great deal to offer the world, even if you don't always appreciate how much. Although you are capable of being shy and introverted on occasions, you are equally likely to be friendly, chatty and very co-operative. You settle to just about any task, though you do possess a sense of freedom that makes it difficult for you to be cooped up in the same place for days and weeks at a stretch. You prefer the sort of tasks that allow your own natural proclivities to shine out, and you exhibit an instinctive creative tendency in almost anything you do.

Use your natural popularity to the full. People are always willing to put themselves out on your behalf, mainly because they know how generous you are and want to repay you for some previous favour. You should never be too proud to accept this sort of proffered help and must avoid running away with the idea that you are unequal to any reasonable task that you set yourself.

It's true that some of your thoughts are extremely deep and that you can get yourself into something of a brown study on occasions, which can be translated by the world around you as depression. However, you are far more stable than you probably believe yourself to be because Pisces is actually one of the toughest of the zodiac signs.

Because you are born of a Water sign it is likely that you would take great delight in living near the sea, or some other large body of water. This isn't essential to your well-being but it does feed your imagination. The vastness of nature in all its forms probably appeals to you in any case and most Pisceans love the natural world with its staggering diversity.

In love you are ardent and sincere, but you do need to make sure that you choose the right individual to suit you. Pisceans often settle for a protecting arm, but if this turns out to be stifling, trouble could follow. You would find it hard to live with anyone who didn't have at least a degree of your sensitivity, and you need a partner who will allow you to retain that sense of inner freedom that is so vital to your well-being.

Make the most of the many gifts and virtues that nature has bestowed upon you and don't be afraid to let people know what you really are. Actually establishing this in the first place isn't easy for you. Pisceans respond well to almost any form of meditation, which is not surprising because the sign of the Fishes is the most spiritually motivated zodiac sign of them all. When you know yourself fully you generate a personality that is an inspiration to everyone.

PISCES ON THE CUSP

Old Moore is often asked how astrological profiles are altered for those people born at either the beginning or the end of a zodiac sign, or, more properly, on the cusps of a sign. In the case of Pisces this would be on the 20th of February and for two or three days after, and similarly at the end of the sign, probably from the 18th to the 20th of March. In this year's Astral Diaries, once again, Old Moore sets out to explain the differences regarding cuspid signs.

The Aquarius Cusp – February 20th to 22nd

This tends to be a generally happy combination of signs, even if some of the people you come into contact with find you rather difficult to understand from time to time. You are quite capable of cutting a dash, as any Aquarian would be, and yet at the same time you have the quiet and contemplative qualities more typified by Pisces. You tend to be seen as an immensely attractive person, even if you are the last one in the world to accept this fact. People find you to be friendly, very approachable and good company in almost any social or personal setting. It isn't hard for you to get on with others, though since you are not so naturally quiet as Pisces when taken alone, you are slightly more willing to speak your mind and to help out, though usually in a very diplomatic manner.

At work you are very capable and many people with this combination find themselves working on behalf of humanity as a whole. Thus work in social services, hospitals or charities really suits the unique combinations thrown up by this sign mixture. Management is right up your street, though there are times when your conception of popularity takes the foremost place in your mind. Occasionally this could take the edge off executive decisions. A careful attention to detail shows you in a position to get things done, even jobs that others shun. You don't really care for getting your hands dirty but will tackle almost any task if you know it to be necessary. Being basically self-sufficient, you also love the company of others, and it is this adaptability that is the hallmark of success to Aquarian-cusp Pisceans.

Few people actually know you as well as they think they do because the waters of your nature run quite deep. Your real task in life is to let the world know how you feel, something you fight shy of doing now and again. There are positive gains in your life, brought about as a result of your adaptable and pleasing nature. Aquarius present in the nature allows Pisces to act at its best.

The Aries Cusp – March 18th to 20th

This is a Piscean with attitude and probably one of the most difficult zodiac sign combinations to be understood, not only by those people with whom you come into contact but clearly by yourself too. If there are any problems thrown up here they come from the fact that Pisces and Aries have such different ways of expressing themselves to the world at large. Aries is very upfront, dynamic and dominant, all factors that are simply diametrically opposed to the way Pisces thinks and behaves. So the real task in life is to find ways to combine the qualities of Pisces and Aries, in a way that suits the needs of both and without becoming totally confused with regard to your basic nature.

The problem is usually solved by a compartmentation of life. For example, many people with this combination will show the Aries qualities strongly at work, whilst dropping into the Piscean mode socially and at home. This may invariably be the case but there are bound to be times when the underlying motivations become mixed, which can confuse those with whom you come into contact.

Having said all of this you can be the least selfish and most successful individual when you are fighting for the rights of others. This is the zodiac combination of the true social reformer, the genuine politician and the committed pacifist. It seems paradoxical to suggest that someone could fight tenaciously for peace, but this is certainly true in your case. You have excellent executive skills and yet retain an ability to tell other people what they should be doing, in fairly strident terms, usually without upsetting anyone. There is a degree of genuine magic about you that makes you very attractive and there is likely to be more than one love affair in your life. A steadfast view of romance may not be naturally present within your basic nature but like so much else you can 'train' this quality into existence.

Personal success is likely, but it probably doesn't matter all that much in a material sense. The important thing to you is being needed by the world at large.

PISCES AND ITS ASCENDANTS

The nature of every individual on the planet is composed of the rich variety of zodiac signs and planetary positions that were present at the time of their birth. Your Sun sign, which in your case is Pisces, is one of the many factors when it comes to assessing the unique person you are. Probably the most important consideration, other than your Sun sign, is to establish the zodiac sign that was rising over the eastern horizon at the time that you were born. This is your Ascending or Rising sign. Most popular astrology fails to take account of the Ascendant, and yet its importance remains with you from the very moment of your birth, through every day of your life. The Ascendant is evident in the way you approach the world, and so, when meeting a person for the first time, it is this astrological influence that you are most likely to notice first. Our Ascending sign essentially represents what we appear to be, while the Sun sign is what we feel inside ourselves.

The Ascendant also has the potential for modifying our overall nature. For example, if you were born at a time of day when Pisces was passing over the eastern horizon (this would be around the time of dawn) then you would be classed as a double Pisces. As such, you would typify this zodiac sign, both internally and in your dealings with others. However, if your Ascendant sign turned out to be a Fire sign, such as Aries, there would be a profound alteration of nature, away from the expected qualities of Pisces.

One of the reasons why popular astrology often ignores the Ascendant is that it has always been rather difficult to establish. Old Moore has found a way to make this possible by devising an easy-to-use table, which you will find on page 125 of this book. Using this, you can establish your Ascendant sign at a glance. You will need to know your rough time of birth, then it is simply a case of following the instructions.

For those readers who have no idea of their time of birth it might be worth allowing a good friend, or perhaps your partner, to read through the section that follows this introduction. Someone who deals with you on a regular basis may easily discover your Ascending sign, even though you could have some difficulty establishing it for yourself. A good understanding of this component of your nature is essential if you want to be aware of that 'other person' who is responsible for the way you make contact with the world at large. Your Sun sign, Ascendant sign, and the other pointers in this book will, together, allow you a far better understanding of what makes you tick as an individual. Peeling back the different layers of your astrological make-up can be an enlightening experience, and the Ascendant may represent one of the most important layers of all.

Pisces with Pisces Ascendant

You are a kind and considerate person who would do almost anything to please the people around you. Creative and extremely perceptive, nobody knows the twists and turns of human nature better than you do, and you make it your business to serve humanity in any way you can. Not everyone understands what makes you tick, and part of the reason for this state of affairs is that you are often not really quite 'in' the world as much as the people you encounter in a day-to-day sense. At work you are generally cheerful, though you can be very quiet on occasions, but since you are consistent in this regard, you don't attract adverse attention or accusations of being moody, as some other variants of Pisces sometimes do. Confusion can beset you on occasions, especially when you are trying to reconcile your own opposing needs. There are certain moments of discontent to be encountered which so often come from trying to please others, even when to do so goes against your own instincts.

As age and experience add to your personal armoury you relax more with the world and find yourself constantly sought out for words of wisdom. The vast majority of people care for you deeply.

Pisces with Aries Ascendant

Although not an easy combination to deal with, the Pisces with an Aries Ascendant does bring something very special to the world in the way of natural understanding allied to practical assistance. It's true that you can sometimes be a dreamer, but there is nothing wrong with that as long as you have the ability to turn some of your wishes into reality, and this you are usually able to do, often for the sake of those around you. Conversation comes easily to you, though you also possess a slightly wistful and poetic side to your nature, which is attractive to the many people who call you a friend. A natural entertainer, you bring a sense of the comic to the often serious qualities of Aries, though without losing the determination that typifies the sign.

In relationships you are ardent, sincere and supportive, with a social conscience that sometimes finds you fighting the battles of the less privileged members of society. Family is important to you and this is a combination that invariably leads to parenthood. Away from the cut and thrust of everyday life you relax more fully, and think about matters more deeply than more typical Aries types might.

Pisces with Taurus Ascendant

You are clearly a very sensitive type of person and that sometimes makes it rather difficult for others to know how they might best approach you. Private and deep, you are nevertheless socially inclined on many occasions. However, because your nature is bottomless it is possible that some types would actually accuse you of being shallow. How can this come about? Well, it's simple really. The fact is that you rarely show anyone what is going on in the deepest recesses of your mind and so your responses can appear to be trite or even ill-considered. This is far from the truth, as those who are allowed into the 'inner sanctum' would readily admit. You are something of a sensualist, and relish staying in bed late and simply pleasing yourself for days on end. However, you have Taurean traits so you desire a tidy environment in which to live your usually long life.

You are able to deal with the routine aspects of life quite well and can be a capable worker once you are up and firing on all cylinders. It is very important that you maintain an interest in what you are doing, because the recesses of your dreamy mind can sometimes appear to be infinitely more attractive. Your imagination is second to none and this fact can often be turned to your advantage.

Pisces with Gemini Ascendant

There is great duality inherent in this combination, and sometimes this can cause a few problems. Part of the trouble stems from the fact that you often fail to realise what you want from life, and you could also be accused of failing to take the time out to think things through carefully enough. You are reactive, and although you have every bit of the natural charm that typifies the sign of Gemini, you are more prone to periods of self-doubt and confusion. However, you should not allow these facts to get you down too much, because you are also genuinely loved and have a tremendous capacity to look after others, a factor which is more important to you than any other. It's true that personal relationships can sometimes be a cause of difficulty for you, partly because your constant need to know what makes other people tick could drive them up the wall. Accepting people at face value seems to be the best key to happiness of a personal sort, and there are occasions when your very real and natural intuition has to be put on hold.

It's likely that you are an original, particularly in the way you dress. An early rebellious stage often gives way to a more comfortable form of eccentricity. When you are at your best, just about everyone adores you.

Pisces with Cancer Ascendant

A deep, double Water-sign combination this, and it might serve to make you a very misunderstood, though undoubtedly popular, individual. You are anxious to make a good impression, probably too keen under certain circumstances, and you do everything you can to help others, even if you don't know them very well. It's true that you are deeply sensitive and quite easily brought to tears by the suffering of this most imperfect world that we inhabit. Fatigue can be a problem, though this is somewhat nullified by the fact that you can withdraw completely into the deep recesses of your own mind when it becomes necessary to do so.

You may not be the most gregarious person in the world, simply because it isn't easy for you to put some of your most important considerations into words. This is easier when you are in the company of people you know and trust, though even trust is a commodity that is difficult for you to find, particularly since you may have been hurt by being too willing to share your thoughts early in life. With age comes wisdom and maturity, and the older you are, the better you will learn to handle this potent and demanding combination. You will never go short of either friends or would-be lovers, and may be one of the most magnetic types of both Cancer and Pisces.

Pisces with Leo Ascendant

You are a very sensitive soul, on occasions too much so for your own good. However, there is not a better advocate for the rights of humanity than you represent and you constantly do what you can to support the downtrodden and oppressed. Good causes are your thing and there are likely to be many in your life. You will probably find yourself pushed to the front of almost any enterprise of which you are a part because, despite the deeper qualities of Pisces, you are a natural leader. Even on those occasions when it feels as though you lack confidence, you manage to muddle through somehow and your smile is as broad as the day. Few sign combinations are more loved than this one, mainly because you do not have a malicious bone in your body, and will readily forgive and forget, which the Lion on its own often will not.

Although you are capable of acting on impulse, you do so from a deep sense of moral conviction, so that most of your endeavours are designed to suit other people too. They recognise this fact and will push much support back in your direction. Even when you come across troubles in your life you manage to find ways to sort them out, and will invariably notice something new to smile about on the way. Your sensitivity rating is massive and you can easily be moved to tears.

Pisces with Virgo Ascendant

You might have been accused on occasions of being too sensitive for your own good, a charge that is not entirely without foundation. Certainly you are very understanding of the needs of others, sometimes to the extent that you put everything aside to help them. This would also be true in the case of charities, for you care very much about the world and the people who cling tenaciously to its surface. Your ability to love on a one-to-one basis knows no bounds, though you may not discriminate as much as you could, particularly when young, and might have one or two false starts in the love stakes. You don't always choose to verbalise your thoughts and this can cause problems, because there is always so much going on in your mind and Virgo especially needs good powers of communication. Pisces is quieter and you need to force yourself to say what you think when the explanation is important.

You would never betray a confidence and sometimes take on rather more for the sake of your friends than is strictly good for you. This is not a fault but can cause you problems all the same. Because you are so intuitive there is little that escapes your attention, though you should avoid being pessimistic about your insights. Changes of scenery suit you and travel would bring out the best in what can be a repressed nature.

Pisces with Libra Ascendant

An Air and Water combination, you are not easy to understand and have depths that show at times, surprising those people who thought they already knew what you were. You will always keep people guessing and are just as likely to hitchhike around Europe as you are to hold down a steady job, both of which you would undertake with the same degree of commitment and success. Usually young at heart, but always carrying the potential for an old head on young shoulders, you are something of a paradox and not at all easy for totally 'straight' types to understand. But you always make an impression, and tend to be very attractive to members of the opposite sex.

In matters of health you do have to be a little careful because you dissipate much nervous energy and can sometimes be inclined to push yourself too hard, at least in a mental sense. Frequent periods of rest and meditation will do you the world of good and should improve your level of wisdom, which tends to be fairly high already. Much of your effort in life is expounded on behalf of humanity as a whole, for you care deeply, love totally and always give of your best. Whatever your faults and failings might be, you are one of the most popular people around.

Pisces with Scorpio Ascendant

You stand a chance of disappearing so deep into yourself that other people would need one of those long ladders that cave explorers use to even find you. It isn't really your fault, because both Scorpio and Pisces, as Water signs, are difficult to understand and you have them both. But that doesn't mean that you should be content to remain in the dark, and the warmth of your nature is all you need to shine a light on the wonderful qualities you possess. But the primary word of warning is that you must put yourself on display and allow others to know what you are, before their appreciation of these facts becomes apparent.

As a server of the world you are second to none and it is hard to find a person with this combination who is not, in some way, looking out for the people around them. Immensely attractive to others, you are also one of the most sought-after lovers. Much of this has to do with your deep and abiding charm, but the air of mystery that surrounds you also helps. Some of you will marry too early, and end up regretting the fact, though the majority of people with Scorpio and Pisces will find the love they deserve in the end. You are able, just, firm but fair, though a sucker for a hard luck story and as kind as the day is long. It's hard to imagine how so many good points could be ignored by others.

Pisces with Sagittarius Ascendant

A very attractive combination this, because the more dominant qualities of the Archer are somehow mellowed-out by the caring Water-sign qualities of the Fishes. You can be very outgoing, but there is always a deeper side to your nature that allows others to know that you are thinking about them. Few people could fall out with either your basic nature or your attitude to the world at large, even though there are depths to your nature that may not be easily understood. You are capable, have a good executive ability and can work hard to achieve your objectives, even if you get a little disillusioned on the way. Much of your life is given over to helping those around you and there is a great tendency for you to work for and on behalf of humanity as a whole. A sense of community is brought to most of what you do and you enjoy co-operation. Although you have the natural ability to attract people to you, the Pisces half of your nature makes you just a little more reserved in personal matters than might otherwise be the case. More careful in your choices than either sign taken alone, you still have to make certain that your motivations when commencing a personal relationship are the right ones. You love to be happy, and to offer gifts of happiness to others.

Pisces with Capricorn Ascendant

You are certainly not the easiest person in the world to understand, mainly because your nature is so deep and your personality so complicated, that others are somewhat intimidated at the prospect of staring into this abyss. All the same your friendly nature is attractive, and there will always be people around who are fascinated by the sheer magnetic quality that is intrinsic to this zodiac mix. Sentimental and extremely kind, there is no limit to the extent of your efforts on behalf of a deserving world, though there are some people around who wonder at your commitment and who may ridicule you a little for your staying-power, even in the face of some adversity. At work you are very capable, will work long and hard, and can definitely expect a greater degree of financial and practical success than Pisces when taken alone. Routines don't bother you too much, though you do need regular periods of introspection, which help to recharge low batteries and a battered self-esteem. In affairs of the heart you are given to impulse, which belies the more careful qualities of Capricorn. However, the determination remains intact and you are quite capable of chasing rainbows round and round the same field, never realising that you can't get to the end of them. Generally speaking you are an immensely lovable person and a great favourite to many.

Pisces with Aquarius Ascendant

Here we find the originality of Aquarius balanced by the very sensitive qualities of Pisces, and it makes for a very interesting combination. When it comes to understanding other people you are second to none, but it's certain that you are more instinctive than either Pisces or Aquarius when taken alone. You are better at routines than Aquarius, but also relish a challenge more than the typical Piscean would. Active and enterprising, you tend to know what you want from life, but consideration of others, and the world at large, will always be part of the scenario. People with this combination often work on behalf of humanity and are to be found in social work, the medical profession and religious institutions. As far as beliefs are concerned you don't conform to established patterns, and yet may get closer to the truth of the Creator than many deep theological thinkers have ever been able to do. Acting on impulse as much as you do means that not everyone understands the way your mind works, but your popularity will invariably see you through.

Passionate and deeply sensitive, you are able to negotiate the twists and turns of a romantic life that is hardly likely to be run-of-the-mill. In the end, however, you should certainly be able to find a very deep personal and spiritual happiness.

THE MOON AND THE PART IT PLAYS IN YOUR LIFE

In astrology the Moon is probably the single most important heavenly body after the Sun. Its unique position, as partner to the Earth on its journey around the solar system, means that the Moon appears to pass through the signs of the zodiac extremely quickly. The zodiac position of the Moon at the time of your birth plays a great part in personal character and is especially significant in the build-up of your emotional nature.

Sun Moon Cycles

The first lunar cycle deals with the part the position of the Moon plays relative to your Sun sign. I have made the fluctuations of this pattern easy for you to understand by means of a simple cyclic graph. It appears on the first page of each 'Your Month At A Glance', under the title 'Highs and Lows'. The graph displays the lunar cycle and you will soon learn to understand how its movements have a bearing on your level of energy and your abilities.

Your Own Moon Sign

Discovering the position of the Moon at the time of your birth has always been notoriously difficult because tracking the complex zodiac positions of the Moon is not easy. This process has been reduced to three simple stages with Old Moore's unique Lunar Tables. A breakdown of the Moon's zodiac positions can be found from page 28 onwards, so that once you know what your Moon Sign is, you can see what part this plays in the overall build-up of your personal character.

If you follow the instructions on the next page you will soon be able to work out exactly what zodiac sign the Moon occupied on the day that you were born and you can then go on to compare the reading for this position with those of your Sun sign and your Ascendant. It is partly the comparison between these three important positions that goes towards making you the unique individual you are.

HOW TO DISCOVER YOUR MOON SIGN

This is a three-stage process. You may need a pen and a piece of paper but if you follow the instructions below the process should only take a minute or so.

STAGE 1 First of all you need to know the Moon Age at the time of your birth. If you look at Moon Table 1, on page 26, you will find all the years between 1917 and 2015 down the left side. Find the year of your birth and then trace across to the right to the month of your birth. Where the two intersect you will find a number. This is the date of the New Moon in the month that you were born. You now need to count forward the number of days between the New Moon and your own birthday. For example, if the New Moon in the month of your birth was shown as being the 6th and you were born on the 20th, your Moon Age Day would be 14. If the New Moon in the month of your birth came after your birthday, you need to count forward from the New Moon in the previous month. If you were born in a Leap Year, remember to count the 29th February. You can tell if your birth year was a Leap Year if the last two digits can be divided by four. Whatever the result, jot this number down so that you do not forget it.

STAGE 2 Take a look at Moon Table 2 on page 27. Down the left hand column look for the date of your birth. Now trace across to the month of your birth. Where the two meet you will find a letter. Copy this letter down alongside your Moon Age Day.

STAGE 3 Moon Table 3 on page 27 will supply you with the zodiac sign the Moon occupied on the day of your birth. Look for your Moon Age Day down the left hand column and then for the letter you found in Stage 2. Where the two converge you will find a zodiac sign and this is the sign occupied by the Moon on the day that you were born.

Your Zodiac Moon Sign Explained

You will find a profile of all zodiac Moon Signs on pages 28 to 31, showing in yet another way how astrology helps to make you into the individual that you are. In each daily entry of the Astral Diary you can find the zodiac position of the Moon for every day of the year. This also allows you to discover your lunar birthdays. Since the Moon passes through all the signs of the zodiac in about a month, you can expect something like twelve lunar birthdays each year. At these times you are likely to be emotionally steady and able to make the sort of decisions that have real, lasting value.

Moon Table 1

YEAR	JAN	FEB	MAR	YEAR	JAN	FEB	MAR	YEAR	JAN	FEB	MAR
1917	24	22	23	1950	18	16	18	1983	14	13	14
1918	12	11	12	1951	7	6	7	1984	3	1	2
1919	1/31	–	2/31	1952	26	25	25	1985	21	19	21
1920	21	19	20	1953	15	14	15	1986	10	9	10
1921	9	8	9	1954	5	3	5	1987	29	28	29
1922	27	26	28	1955	24	22	24	1988	18	17	18
1923	17	15	17	1956	13	11	12	1989	7	6	7
1924	6	5	5	1957	1/30	–	1/31	1990	26	25	26
1925	24	23	24	1958	19	18	20	1991	15	14	15
1926	14	12	14	1959	9	7	9	1992	4	3	4
1927	3	2	3	1960	27	26	27	1993	24	22	24
1928	21	19	21	1961	16	15	16	1994	11	10	12
1929	11	9	11	1962	6	5	6	1995	1/31	–	1/30
1930	29	28	30	1963	25	23	25	1996	19	18	19
1931	18	17	19	1964	14	13	14	1997	9	7	9
1932	7	6	7	1965	3	1	2	1998	27	26	27
1933	25	24	26	1966	21	19	21	1999	16	15	16
1934	15	14	15	1967	10	9	10	2000	6	4	6
1935	5	3	5	1968	29	28	29	2001	24	23	25
1936	24	22	23	1969	19	17	18	2002	13	12	13
1937	12	11	12	1970	7	6	7	2003	3	1	2
1938	1/31	–	2/31	1971	26	25	26	2004	21	20	21
1939	20	19	20	1972	15	14	15	2005	10	9	10
1940	9	8	9	1973	5	4	5	2006	29	28	29
1941	27	26	27	1974	24	22	24	2007	18	16	18
1942	16	15	16	1975	12	11	12	2008	8	6	7
1943	6	4	6	1976	1/31	29	30	2009	26	25	26
1944	25	24	24	1977	19	18	19	2010	15	14	15
1945	14	12	14	1978	9	7	9	2011	4	3	5
1946	3	2	3	1979	27	26	27	2012	23	22	22
1947	21	19	21	1980	16	15	16	2013	12	10	12
1948	11	9	11	1981	6	4	6	2014	1/31	–	1
1949	29	27	29	1982	25	23	24	2015	19	20	19

Table 2

DAY	FEB	MAR
1	D	F
2	D	G
3	D	G
4	D	G
5	D	G
6	D	G
7	D	G
8	D	G
9	D	G
10	E	G
11	E	G
12	E	H
13	E	H
14	E	H
15	E	H
16	E	H
17	E	H
18	E	H
19	E	H
20	F	H
21	F	H
22	F	I
23	F	I
24	F	I
25	F	I
26	F	I
27	F	I
28	F	I
29	F	I
30	–	I
31	–	I

Table 3

M/D	D	E	F	G	H	I	J
0	AQ	PI	PI	PI	AR	AR	AR
1	PI	PI	PI	AR	AR	AR	TA
2	PI	PI	AR	AR	AR	TA	TA
3	PI	AR	AR	AR	TA	TA	TA
4	AR	AR	AR	TA	TA	GE	GE
5	AR	TA	TA	TA	GE	GE	GE
6	TA	TA	TA	GE	GE	GE	CA
7	TA	TA	GE	GE	GE	CA	CA
8	TA	GE	GE	GE	CA	CA	CA
9	GE	GE	CA	CA	CA	CA	LE
10	GE	CA	CA	CA	LE	LE	LE
11	CA	CA	CA	LE	LE	LE	VI
12	CA	CA	LE	LE	LE	VI	VI
13	LE	LE	LE	LE	VI	VI	VI
14	LE	LE	VI	VI	VI	LI	LI
15	LE	VI	VI	VI	LI	LI	LI
16	VI	VI	VI	LI	LI	LI	SC
17	VI	VI	LI	LI	LI	SC	SC
18	VI	LI	LI	LI	SC	SC	SC
19	LI	LI	LI	SC	SC	SC	SA
20	LI	SC	SC	SC	SA	SA	SA
21	SC	SC	SC	SA	SA	SA	CP
22	SC	SC	SA	SA	SA	CP	CP
23	SC	SA	SA	SA	CP	CP	CP
24	SA	SA	SA	CP	CP	CP	AQ
25	SA	CP	CP	CP	AQ	AQ	AQ
26	CP	CP	CP	AQ	AQ	AQ	PI
27	CP	AQ	AQ	AQ	AQ	PI	PI
28	AQ	AQ	AQ	AQ	PI	PI	PI
29	AQ	AQ	AQ	PI	PI	PI	AR

AR = Aries, TA = Taurus, GE = Gemini, CA = Cancer, LE = Leo, VI = Virgo, LI = Libra, SC = Scorpio, SA = Sagittarius, CP = Capricorn, AQ = Aquarius, PI = Pisces

MOON SIGNS

Moon in Aries

You have a strong imagination, courage, determination and a desire to do things in your own way and forge your own path through life.

Originality is a key attribute; you are seldom stuck for ideas although your mind is changeable and you could take the time to focus on individual tasks. Often quick-tempered, you take orders from few people and live life at a fast pace. Avoid health problems by taking regular time out for rest and relaxation.

Emotionally, it is important that you talk to those you are closest to and work out your true feelings. Once you discover that people are there to help, there is less necessity for you to do everything yourself.

Moon in Taurus

The Moon in Taurus gives you a courteous and friendly manner, which means you are likely to have many friends.

The good things in life mean a lot to you, as Taurus is an Earth sign that delights in experiences which please the senses. Hence you are probably a lover of good food and drink, which may in turn mean you need to keep an eye on the bathroom scales, especially as looking good is also important to you.

Emotionally you are fairly stable and you stick by your own standards. Taureans do not respond well to change. Intuition also plays an important part in your life.

Moon in Gemini

You have a warm-hearted character, sympathetic and eager to help others. At times reserved, you can also be articulate and chatty: this is part of the paradox of Gemini, which always brings duplicity to the nature. You are interested in current affairs, have a good intellect, and are good company and likely to have many friends. Most of your friends have a high opinion of you and would be ready to defend you should the need arise. However, this is usually unnecessary, as you are quite capable of defending yourself in any verbal confrontation.

Travel is important to your inquisitive mind and you find intellectual stimulus in mixing with people from different cultures. You also gain much from reading, writing and the arts but you do need plenty of rest and relaxation in order to avoid fatigue.

Moon in Cancer

The Moon in Cancer at the time of birth is a fortunate position as Cancer is the Moon's natural home. This means that the qualities of compassion and understanding given by the Moon are especially enhanced in your nature, and you are friendly and sociable and cope well with emotional pressures. You cherish home and family life, and happily do the domestic tasks. Your surroundings are important to you and you hate squalor and filth. You are likely to have a love of music and poetry.

Your basic character, although at times changeable like the Moon itself, depends on symmetry. You aim to make your surroundings comfortable and harmonious, for yourself and those close to you.

Moon in Leo

The best qualities of the Moon and Leo come together to make you warmhearted, fair, ambitious and self-confident. With good organisational abilities, you invariably rise to a position of responsibility in your chosen career. This is fortunate as you don't enjoy being an 'also-ran' and would rather be an important part of a small organisation than a menial in a large one.

You should be lucky in love, and happy, provided you put in the effort to make a comfortable home for yourself and those close to you. It is likely that you will have a love of pleasure, sport, music and literature. Life brings you many rewards, most of them as a direct result of your own efforts, although you may be luckier than average and ready to make the best of any situation.

Moon in Virgo

You are endowed with good mental abilities and a keen receptive memory, but you are never ostentatious or pretentious. Naturally quite reserved, you still have many friends, especially of the opposite sex. Marital relationships must be discussed carefully and worked at so that they remain harmonious, as personal attachments can be a problem if you do not give them your full attention.

Talented and persevering, you possess artistic qualities and are a good homemaker. Earning your honours through genuine merit, you work long and hard towards your objectives but show little pride in your achievements. Many short journeys will be undertaken in your life.

Moon in Libra

With the Moon in Libra you are naturally popular and make friends easily. People like you, probably more than you realise, you bring fun to a party and are a natural diplomat. For all its good points, Libra is not the most stable of astrological signs and, as a result, your emotions can be a little unstable too. Therefore, although the Moon in Libra is said to be good for love and marriage, your Sun sign and Rising sign will have an important effect on your emotional and loving qualities.

You must remember to relate to others in your decision-making. Co-operation is crucial because Libra represents the 'balance' of life that can only be achieved through harmonious relationships. Conformity is not easy for you because Libra, an Air sign, likes its independence.

Moon in Scorpio

Some people might call you pushy. In fact, all you really want to do is to live life to the full and protect yourself and your family from the pressures of life. Take care to avoid giving the impression of being sarcastic or impulsive and use your energies wisely and constructively.

You have great courage and you invariably achieve your goals by force of personality and sheer effort. You are fond of mystery and are good at predicting the outcome of situations and events. Travel experiences can be beneficial to you.

You may experience problems if you do not take time to examine your motives in a relationship, and also if you allow jealousy, always a feature of Scorpio, to cloud your judgement.

Moon in Sagittarius

The Moon in Sagittarius helps to make you a generous individual with humanitarian qualities and a kind heart. Restlessness may be intrinsic as your mind is seldom still. Perhaps because of this, you have a need for change that could lead you to several major moves during your adult life. You are not afraid to stand your ground when you know your judgement is right, you speak directly and have good intuition.

At work you are quick, efficient and versatile and so you make an ideal employee. You need work to be intellectually demanding and do not enjoy tedious routines.

In relationships, you anger quickly if faced with stupidity or deception, though you are just as quick to forgive and forget. Emotionally, there are times when your heart rules your head.

Moon in Capricorn

The Moon in Capricorn makes you popular and likely to come into the public eye in some way. The watery Moon is not entirely comfortable in the Earth sign of Capricorn and this may lead to some difficulties in the early years of life. An initial lack of creative ability and indecision must be overcome before the true qualities of patience and perseverance inherent in Capricorn can show through.

You have good administrative ability and are a capable worker, and if you are careful you can accumulate wealth. But you must be cautious and take professional advice in partnerships, as you are open to deception. You may be interested in social or welfare work, which suit your organisational skills and sympathy for others.

Moon in Aquarius

The Moon in Aquarius makes you an active and agreeable person with a friendly, easy-going nature. Sympathetic to the needs of others, you flourish in a laid-back atmosphere. You are broad-minded, fair and open to suggestion, although sometimes you have an unconventional quality which others can find hard to understand.

You are interested in the strange and curious, and in old articles and places. You enjoy trips to these places and gain much from them. Political, scientific and educational work interests you and you might choose a career in science or technology.

Money-wise, you make gains through innovation and concentration and Lunar Aquarians often tackle more than one job at a time. In love you are kind and honest.

Moon in Pisces

You have a kind, sympathetic nature, somewhat retiring at times, but you always take account of others' feelings and help when you can.

Personal relationships may be problematic, but as life goes on you can learn from your experiences and develop a better understanding of yourself and the world around you.

You have a fondness for travel, appreciate beauty and harmony and hate disorder and strife. You may be fond of literature and would make a good writer or speaker yourself. You have a creative imagination and may come across as an incurable romantic. You have strong intuition, maybe bordering on a mediumistic quality, which sets you apart from the mass. You may not be rich in cash terms, but your personal gifts are worth more than gold.

PISCES IN LOVE

Discover how compatible in love you are with people from the same and other signs of the zodiac. Five stars equals a match made in heaven!

Pisces meets Pisces

Pisceans are easy-going and get on well with most people, so when two Pisceans get together, harmony is invariably the result. While this isn't the most dynamic relationship, there is mutual understanding, and a desire to please on both sides. Neither partner is likely to be overbearing or selfish. Family responsibilities should be happily shared and home surroundings will be comfortable, but never pretentious. One of the better pairings for the sign of the Fishes. Star rating: *****

Pisces meets Aries

Still waters run deep, and they don't come much deeper than Pisces. Although these signs share the same quadrant of the zodiac, they have little in common. Pisces is a dreamer, a romantic idealist with steady and spiritual goals. Aries needs to be on the move, and has very different ideals. It's hard to see how a relationship could develop but, with patience, there is a chance that things might work out. Pisces needs incentive, and Aries may be the sign to offer it. Star rating: **

Pisces meets Taurus

No problem here, unless both parties come from the quieter side of their respective signs. Most of the time Taurus and Pisces would live comfortably together, offering mutual support and deep regard. Taurus can offer the personal qualities that Pisces craves, whilst Pisces understands and copes with the Bull's slightly stubborn qualities. Taurus is likely to travel in Piscean company, so there is a potential for wide-ranging experiences and variety which is essential. There will be some misunderstandings, mainly because Pisces is so deep, but that won't prevent their enduring happiness. Star rating: ***

Pisces meets Gemini

Gemini likes to think of itself as intuitive and intellectual, but it will never understand Pisces' dark depths. Another stumbling block is that both Gemini and Pisces are 'split' signs – the Twins and the two Fishes – which means that both are capable of dual personalities. There won't be any shortage of affection, but the real question has to be how much these people feel they have in common. Pisces is extremely kind, and so is Gemini most of the time. But Pisces does too much soul-searching for Gemini, who might eventually become bored. Star rating: ★★★

Pisces meets Cancer

This is likely to be a very successful match. Cancer and Pisces are both Water signs, both deep, sensitive and very caring. Pisces loves deeply, and Cancer wants to be loved. There will be few fireworks here, and a very quiet house. But that doesn't mean that either love or action is lacking – the latter of which is just behind closed doors. Family and children are important to both signs and both are prepared to work hard, but Pisces is the more restless of the two and needs the support and security that Cancer offers. Star rating: ★★★★★

Pisces meets Leo

Pisces always needs to understand others, which makes Leo feel warm and loved, while Leo sees, to its delight, that Pisces needs to be protected and taken care of. Pisceans are often lacking in self-confidence which is something Leo has to spare, and happily it is often infectious. Pisces' inevitable cares are swept away on a tide of Leonine cheerfulness. This couple's home would be cheerful and full of love, which is beneficial to all family members. This is not a meeting of minds, but rather an understanding and appreciation of differences. Star rating: ★★★★

Pisces meets Virgo

This looks an unpromising match from beginning to end. There are exceptions to every rule, particularly where Pisces is concerned, but these two signs are both so deep it's hard to imagine that they could ever find what makes the other tick. The depth is different in each case: Virgo's ruminations are extremely materialistic, while Pisces exists in a world of deep-felt, poorly expressed emotion. Pisces and Virgo might find they don't talk much, so only in a contemplative, almost monastic, match would they ever get on. Still, in a vast zodiac, anything is possible. Star rating: **

Pisces meets Libra

Libra and Pisces can be extremely fond of each other, even deeply in love, but this alone isn't a stable foundation for long-term success. Pisces is extremely deep and doesn't even know itself very well. Libra may initially find this intriguing but will eventually feel frustrated at being unable to understand the Piscean's emotional and personal feelings. Pisces can be jealous and may find Libra's flightiness difficult, which Libra can't stand. They are great friends and they may make it to the romantic stakes, but when they get there a great deal of effort will be necessary. Star rating: ***

Pisces meets Scorpio

If ever there were two zodiac signs that have a total rapport, it has to be Scorpio and Pisces. They share very similar needs: they are not gregarious and are happy with a little silence, good music and time to contemplate the finer things in life, and both are attracted to family life. Apart, they can have a tendency to wander in a romantic sense, but this is reduced when they come together. They are deep, firm friends who enjoy each other's company and this must lead to an excellent chance of success. These people are surely made for each other! Star rating: *****

Pisces meets Sagittarius

Probably the least likely success story for either sign, which is why it scores so low on the star rating. The basic problem is an almost total lack of understanding. A successful relationship needs empathy and progress towards a shared goal but, although both are eager to please, Pisces is too deep and Sagittarius too flighty – they just don't belong on the same planet! As pals, they have more in common and so a friendship is the best hope of success and happiness. Star rating: *

Pisces meets Capricorn

There is some chance of a happy relationship here, but it will need work on both sides. Capricorn is a go-getter, but likes to plan long term. Pisces is naturally more immediate, but has enough intuition to understand the Goat's thinking. Both have patience, but it will usually be Pisces who chooses to play second fiddle. The quiet nature of both signs might be a problem, as someone will have to take the lead, especially in social situations. Both signs should recognise this fact and accommodate it. Star rating: ***

Pisces meets Aquarius

Zodiac signs that follow each other often have something in common, but this is often not the case with Aquarius and Pisces. Both signs are deeply caring, but in different ways. Pisces is one of the deepest zodiac signs, and Aquarius simply isn't prepared to embark on the journey. Pisceans, meanwhile, would probably find Aquarians superficial and even flippant. On the positive side, there is potential for a well-balanced relationship, but unless one party is untypical of their zodiac sign, it often doesn't get started. Star rating: **

VENUS:
THE PLANET OF LOVE

If you look up at the sky around sunset or sunrise you will often see Venus in close attendance to the Sun. It is arguably one of the most beautiful sights of all and there is little wonder that historically it became associated with the goddess of love. But although Venus does play an important part in the way you view love and in the way others see you romantically, this is only one of the spheres of influence that it enjoys in your overall character.

Venus has a part to play in the more cultured side of your life and has much to do with your appreciation of art, literature, music and general creativity. Even the way you look is responsive to the part of the zodiac that Venus occupied at the start of your life, though this fact is also down to your Sun sign and Ascending sign. If, at the time you were born, Venus occupied one of the more gregarious zodiac signs, you will be more likely to wear your heart on your sleeve, as well as to be more attracted to entertainment, social gatherings and good company. If on the other hand Venus occupied a quiet zodiac sign at the time of your birth, you would tend to be more retiring and less willing to shine in public situations.

It's good to know what part the planet Venus plays in your life, for it can have a great bearing on the way you appear to the rest of the world and since we all have to mix with others, you can learn to make the very best of what Venus has to offer you.

One of the great complications in the past has always been trying to establish exactly what zodiac position Venus enjoyed when you were born, because the planet is notoriously difficult to track. However, I have solved that problem by creating a table that is exclusive to your Sun sign, which you will find on the following page.

Establishing your Venus sign could not be easier. Just look up the year of your birth on the page opposite and you will see a sign of the zodiac. This was the sign that Venus occupied in the period covered by your sign in that year. If Venus occupied more than one sign during the period, this is indicated by the date on which the sign changed, and the name of the new sign. For instance, if you were born in 1940, Venus was in Aries until the 9th March, after which time it was in Taurus. If you were born before 9th March your Venus sign is Aries, if you were born on or after 9th March, your Venus sign is Taurus. Once you have established the position of Venus at the time of your birth, you can then look in the pages which follow to see how this has a bearing on your life as a whole.

1917 AQUARIUS / 5.3 PISCES
1918 AQUARIUS
1919 PISCES / 27.2 ARIES
1920 CAPRICORN /
    24.2 AQUARIUS / 19.3 PISCES
1921 ARIES / 8.3 TAURUS
1922 PISCES / 14.3 ARIES
1923 CAPRICORN
1924 ARIES / 10.3 TAURUS
1925 AQUARIUS / 4.3 PISCES
1926 AQUARIUS
1927 PISCES / 26.2 ARIES
1928 CAPRICORN /
    23.2 AQUARIUS / 18.3 PISCES
1929 ARIES / 9.3 TAURUS
1930 PISCES / 13.3 ARIES
1931 CAPRICORN
1932 ARIES / 9.3 TAURUS
1933 AQUARIUS / 4.3 PISCES
1934 AQUARIUS
1935 PISCES / 25.2 ARIES
1936 CAPRICORN /
    23.2 AQUARIUS / 18.3 PISCES
1937 ARIES / 10.3 TAURUS
1938 PISCES / 12.3 ARIES
1939 CAPRICORN
1940 ARIES / 9.3 TAURUS
1941 AQUARIUS / 3.3 PISCES
1942 AQUARIUS
1943 PISCES / 25.2 ARIES
1944 CAPRICORN /
    22.2 AQUARIUS / 18.3 PISCES
1945 ARIES / 11.3 TAURUS
1946 PISCES / 11.3 ARIES
1947 CAPRICORN
1948 ARIES / 8.3 TAURUS
1949 AQUARIUS / 3.3 PISCES
1950 AQUARIUS
1951 PISCES / 24.2 ARIES
1952 CAPRICORN /
    22.2 AQUARIUS / 17.3 PISCES
1953 ARIES
1954 PISCES / 11.3 ARIES
1955 CAPRICORN
1956 ARIES / 8.3 TAURUS
1957 AQUARIUS / 2.3 PISCES
1958 CAPRICORN /
    25.2 AQUARIUS
1959 PISCES / 24.2 ARIES
1960 CAPRICORN /
    21.2 AQUARIUS / 17.3 PISCES
1961 ARIES
1962 PISCES / 10.3 ARIES
1963 CAPRICORN
1964 ARIES / 8.3 TAURUS
1965 AQUARIUS / 1.3 PISCES
1966 AQUARIUS

1967 PISCES / 23.2 ARIES
1968 SAGITTARIUS /
    26.1 CAPRICORN
1969 ARIES
1970 PISCES / 10.3 ARIES
1971 CAPRICORN
1972 ARIES / 7.3 TAURUS
1973 AQUARIUS / 1.3 PISCES
1974 CAPRICORN / 2.3 AQUARIUS
1975 PISCES / 23.2 ARIES
1976 SAGITTARIUS /
    26.1 CAPRICORN
1977 ARIES
1978 PISCES / 9.3 ARIES
1979 CAPRICORN
1980 ARIES / 7.3 TAURUS
1981 AQUARIUS / 28.2 PISCES
1982 CAPRICORN / 4.3 AQUARIUS
1983 PISCES / 23.2 ARIES
1984 SAGITTARIUS /
    25.1 CAPRICORN
1985 ARIES
1986 PISCES / 9.3 ARIES
1987 CAPRICORN
1988 ARIES / 7.3 TAURUS
1989 AQUARIUS / 28.2 PISCES
1990 CAPRICORN / 5.3 AQUARIUS
1991 PISCES / 22.2 ARIES /
    20.3 TAURUS
1992 SAGITTARIUS /
    25.1 CAPRICORN
1993 ARIES
1994 PISCES / 9.3 ARIES
1995 CAPRICORN
1996 ARIES / 7.3 TAURUS
1997 AQUARIUS / 27.2 PISCES
1998 CAPRICORN / 5.3 AQUARIUS
1999 PISCES / 22.2 ARIES /
    19.3 TAURUS
2000 SAGITTARIUS /
    25.1 CAPRICORN
2001 ARIES
2002 PISCES / 9.3 ARIES
2003 CAPRICORN
2004 ARIES / 7.3 TAURUS
2005 AQUARIUS / 27.2 PISCES
2006 CAPRICORN / 5.3 AQUARIUS
2007 PISCES / 22.2 ARIES
2008 SAGITTARIUS /
    25.1 CAPRICORN
2009 ARIES
2010 PISCES / 9.3 ARIES
2011 CAPRICORN
2012 ARIES / 7.3 TAURUS
2013 AQUARIUS / 27.2 PISCES
2014 AQUARIUS / 27.2 PISCES
2015 PISCES / 22.2 ARIES

VENUS THROUGH THE ZODIAC SIGNS

Venus in Aries

Amongst other things, the position of Venus in Aries indicates a fondness for travel, music and all creative pursuits. Your nature tends to be affectionate and you would try not to create confusion or difficulty for others if it could be avoided. Many people with this planetary position have a great love of the theatre, and mental stimulation is of the greatest importance. Early romantic attachments are common with Venus in Aries, so it is very important to establish a genuine sense of romantic continuity. Early marriage is not recommended, especially if it is based on sympathy. You may give your heart a little too readily on occasions.

Venus in Taurus

You are capable of very deep feelings and your emotions tend to last for a very long time. This makes you a trusting partner and lover, whose constancy is second to none. In life you are precise and careful and always try to do things the right way. Although this means an ordered life, which you are comfortable with, it can also lead you to be rather too fussy for your own good. Despite your pleasant nature, you are very fixed in your opinions and quite able to speak your mind. Others are attracted to you and historical astrologers always quoted this position of Venus as being very fortunate in terms of marriage. However, if you find yourself involved in a failed relationship, it could take you a long time to trust again.

Venus in Gemini

As with all associations related to Gemini, you tend to be quite versatile, anxious for change and intelligent in your dealings with the world at large. You may gain money from more than one source but you are equally good at spending it. There is an inference here that you are a good communicator, via either the written or the spoken word, and you love to be in the company of interesting people. Always on the look-out for culture, you may also be very fond of music, and love to indulge the curious and cultured side of your nature. In romance you tend to have more than one relationship and could find yourself associated with someone who has previously been a friend or even a distant relative.

Venus in Cancer

You often stay close to home because you are very fond of family and enjoy many of your most treasured moments when you are with those you love. Being naturally sympathetic, you will always do anything you can to support those around you, even people you hardly know at all. This charitable side of your nature is your most noticeable trait and is one of the reasons why others are naturally so fond of you. Being receptive and in some cases even psychic, you can see through to the soul of most of those with whom you come into contact. You may not commence too many romantic attachments but when you do give your heart, it tends to be unconditionally.

Venus in Leo

It must become quickly obvious to almost anyone you meet that you are kind, sympathetic and yet determined enough to stand up for anyone or anything that is truly important to you. Bright and sunny, you warm the world with your natural enthusiasm and would rarely do anything to hurt those around you, or at least not intentionally. In romance you are ardent and sincere, though some may find your style just a little overpowering. Gains come through your contacts with other people and this could be especially true with regard to romance, for love and money often come hand in hand for those who were born with Venus in Leo. People claim to understand you, though you are more complex than you seem.

Venus in Virgo

Your nature could well be fairly quiet no matter what your Sun sign might be, though this fact often manifests itself as an inner peace and would not prevent you from being basically sociable. Some delays and even the odd disappointment in love cannot be ruled out with this planetary position, though it's a fact that you will usually find the happiness you look for in the end. Catapulting yourself into romantic entanglements that you know to be rather ill-advised is not sensible, and it would be better to wait before you committed yourself exclusively to any one person. It is the essence of your nature to serve the world at large and through doing so it is possible that you will attract money at some stage in your life.

Venus in Libra

Venus is very comfortable in Libra and bestows upon those people who have this planetary position a particular sort of kindness that is easy to recognise. This is a very good position for all sorts of friendships and also for romantic attachments that usually bring much joy into your life. Few individuals with Venus in Libra would avoid marriage and since you are capable of great depths of love, it is likely that you will find a contented personal life. You like to mix with people of integrity and intelligence but don't take kindly to scruffy surroundings or work that means getting your hands too dirty. Careful speculation, good business dealings and money through marriage all seem fairly likely.

Venus in Scorpio

You are quite open and tend to spend money quite freely, even on those occasions when you don't have very much. Although your intentions are always good, there are times when you get yourself in to the odd scrape and this can be particularly true when it comes to romance, which you may come to late or from a rather unexpected direction. Certainly you have the power to be happy and to make others contented on the way, but you find the odd stumbling block on your journey through life and it could seem that you have to work harder than those around you. As a result of this, you gain a much deeper understanding of the true value of personal happiness than many people ever do, and are likely to achieve true contentment in the end.

Venus in Sagittarius

You are lighthearted, cheerful and always able to see the funny side of any situation. These facts enhance your popularity, which is especially high with members of the opposite sex. You should never have to look too far to find romantic interest in your life, though it is just possible that you might be too willing to commit yourself before you are certain that the person in question is right for you. Part of the problem here extends to other areas of life too. The fact is that you like variety in everything and so can tire of situations that fail to offer it. All the same, if you choose wisely and learn to understand your restless side, then great happiness can be yours.

Venus in Capricorn

The most notable trait that comes from Venus in this position is that it makes you trustworthy and able to take on all sorts of responsibilities in life. People are instinctively fond of you and love you all the more because you are always ready to help those who are in any form of need. Social and business popularity can be yours and there is a magnetic quality to your nature that is particularly attractive in a romantic sense. Anyone who wants a partner for a lover, a spouse and a good friend too would almost certainly look in your direction. Constancy is the hallmark of your nature and unfaithfulness would go right against the grain. You might sometimes be a little too trusting.

Venus in Aquarius

This location of Venus offers a fondness for travel and a desire to try out something new at every possible opportunity. You are extremely easy to get along with and tend to have many friends from varied backgrounds, classes and inclinations. You like to live a distinct sort of life and gain a great deal from moving about, both in a career sense and with regard to your home. It is not out of the question that you could form a romantic attachment to someone who comes from far away or be attracted to a person of a distinctly artistic and original nature. What you cannot stand is jealousy, for you have friends of both sexes and would want to keep things that way.

Venus in Pisces

The first thing people tend to notice about you is your wonderful, warm smile. Being very charitable by nature you will do anything to help others, even if you don't know them well. Much of your life may be spent sorting out situations for other people, but it is very important to feel that you are living for yourself too. In the main, you remain cheerful, and tend to be quite attractive to members of the opposite sex. Where romantic attachments are concerned, you could be drawn to people who are significantly older or younger than yourself or to someone with a unique career or point of view. It might be best for you to avoid marrying whilst you are still very young.

HOW THE DIAGRAMS WORK

Through the picture diagrams in the Astral Diary I want to help you to plot your year. With them you can see where the positive and negative aspects will be found in each month. To make the most of them, all you have to do is remember where and when!

Let me show you how they work ...

THE MONTH AT A GLANCE

Just as there are twelve separate zodiac signs, so astrologers believe that each sign has twelve separate aspects to life. Each of the twelve segments relates to a different personal aspect. I list them all every month so that their meanings are always clear.

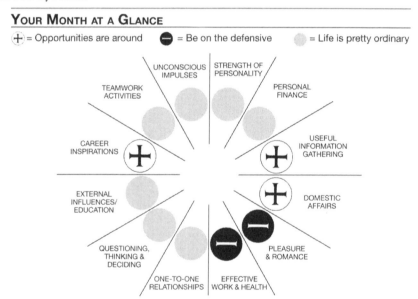

YOUR MONTH AT A GLANCE

⊕ = Opportunities are around ⬤ = Be on the defensive ⬤ = Life is pretty ordinary

- UNCONSCIOUS IMPULSES
- STRENGTH OF PERSONALITY
- TEAMWORK ACTIVITIES
- PERSONAL FINANCE
- CAREER INSPIRATIONS
- USEFUL INFORMATION GATHERING
- EXTERNAL INFLUENCES/ EDUCATION
- DOMESTIC AFFAIRS
- QUESTIONING, THINKING & DECIDING
- PLEASURE & ROMANCE
- ONE-TO-ONE RELATIONSHIPS
- EFFECTIVE WORK & HEALTH

I have designed this chart to show you how and when these twelve different aspects are being influenced throughout the year. When there is a shaded circle, nothing out of the ordinary is to be expected. However, when a circle turns white with a plus sign, the influence is positive. Where the circle is black with a minus sign, it is a negative.

YOUR ENERGY RHYTHM CHART

Below is a picture diagram in which I link your zodiac group to the rhythm of the Moon. In doing this I have calculated when you will be gaining strength from its influence and equally when you may be weakened by it.

If you think of yourself as being like the tides of the ocean then you may understand how your own energies must also rise and fall. And if you understand how it works and when it is working, then you can better organise your activities to achieve more and get things done more easily.

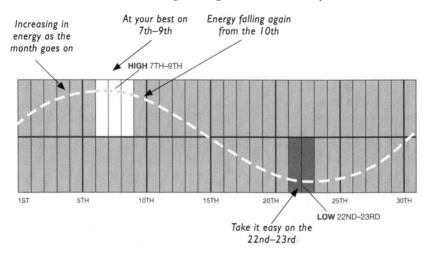

Increasing in energy as the month goes on

At your best on 7th–9th

Energy falling again from the 10th

HIGH 7TH–9TH

1ST   5TH   10TH   15TH   20TH   25TH   30TH

LOW 22ND–23RD

Take it easy on the 22nd–23rd

THE KEY DAYS

Some of the entries are in **bold**, which indicates the working of astrological cycles in your life. Look out for them each week as they are the best days to take action or make decisions. The daily text tells you which area of your life to focus on.

MERCURY RETROGRADE

The Mercury symbol (☿) indicates that Mercury is retrograde on that day. Since Mercury governs communication, the fact that it appears to be moving backwards when viewed from the Earth at this time should warn you that your communication skills are not likely to be at their best and you could expect some setbacks.

PISCES: YOUR YEAR IN BRIEF

If it appears at the beginning of this year that you are not making the progress you would wish, don't worry; this is nothing more than a temporary matter and within a few days everything should be on course again. January and February should find you willing to take on new projects, happy to co-operate with others and quite determined to make headway. Some personal matters could be complicated and a little extra thought will be necessary.

March and April bring you into some small conflicts with family members or friends, though only if you fail to take account of other people's sensibilities. Money matters will be variable at this time, but in the main you will be able to forge ahead in the way that makes you happiest. Don't get hung up on details at this time, but rather look at the bigger picture and plan well ahead. The greater your sense of purpose, the more you will achieve.

Look forward to May and June, two of the most potentially successful months of the year. You may find you are at your effective best and other people are looking upon you very favourably. You may need to be careful about what you are spending, but that's only because there is always a better deal available further down the line. Love looks especially good and may bring contentment at this time.

During July and August you will want to move about as much as possible and would be unlikely to stick fast at anything. Travel of any sort really motivates you and not simply holidays. You can make the very most out of the good weather and may well be undertaking some changes at home with more DIY a definite possibility. Don't be too quick to make up your mind where romance is concerned. If you are looking for love that's fine, but do take your time.

It should become obvious fairly quickly that now is the time to get your plans laid and September and October offer you just the right incentives. Don't get tied up in red tape or routines, and be willing to show a degree of flexibility, especially as far as your personal life is concerned. There could be new incentives that improve your financial standing and maybe even a house move for some.

The last two months of the year, November and December, will find you active, enterprising and probably more relaxed. You know what you want from life and will have a good idea how to get it. Romance looks especially good, as do all relationships, particularly across the Christmas period. Use this to your advantage in number of ways. There is every chance that you will finish the year on a high, but New Year's Eve itself might be quieter than usual.

$\mathcal{J}anuary$

2015

Your Month at a Glance

$\oplus$ = Opportunities are around　　$\ominus$ = Be on the defensive　　● = Life is pretty ordinary

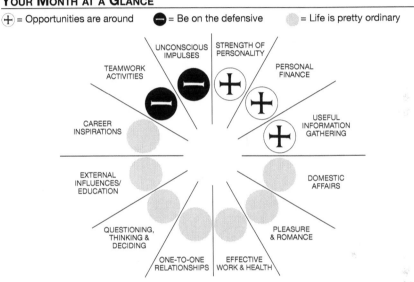

January Highs and Lows

Here I show you how the rhythms of the Moon will affect you this month. Like the tide, your energies and abilities will rise and fall with its pattern. When it is above the centre line, go for it, when it is below, you should be resting.

HIGH 23RD–24TH

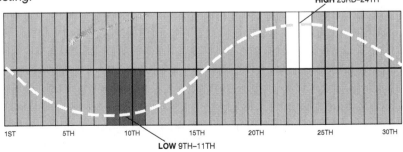

1ST　　5TH　　10TH　　15TH　　20TH　　25TH　　30TH

LOW 9TH–11TH

45

1 THURSDAY
Moon Age Day 11 Moon Sign Taurus

A freedom-loving approach epitomises your attitude and actions on this New Year's Day. You certainly will not take kindly to being fettered in any way and should actively seek any opportunity to ring the changes. Most important of all is your need to travel, even if it is only as far as your local town. Variety is crucial.

2 FRIDAY
Moon Age Day 12 Moon Sign Gemini

A get-together of almost any sort would appeal to you now, especially if it puts you in touch with people you haven't seen for quite a while. It looks as though a good deal of your mind will be focused on the past today and tomorrow, but do remember that the things that really matter lie in the future.

3 SATURDAY
Moon Age Day 13 Moon Sign Gemini

Someone you haven't seen for ages is likely to make a return to your life and this merely emphasises just how much the past is replaying for you at the moment. It's good to meet an old friend, particularly someone who was once so important to you. However, you also need to remind yourself of the importance of today.

4 SUNDAY
Moon Age Day 14 Moon Sign Gemini

You remain serene but happy, and should be able to make much out of what is a generally cold and miserable time of year. You have ways of warming things up, both for yourself and for those around you. Your imagination is also working strongly and will furnish you with ideas of how to entertain people who might be bored.

5 MONDAY
Moon Age Day 15 Moon Sign Cancer

There is a good deal of joy around now, especially where your work is concerned. You can make even the most mundane chores fun and will be doing all you can to lift the spirits of colleagues and friends. Once the working day is over, some special attention directed at your sweetheart or partner would not go amiss.

6 TUESDAY
Moon Age Day 16 Moon Sign Cancer

Now and for the next day or so, you show a strong sense of adventure. It looks as though you would be willing to pit yourself against almost any sort of challenge and you can even show just how courageous Pisces can be. Your attitude might slightly shock friends.

7 WEDNESDAY
Moon Age Day 17 Moon Sign Leo

Life is likely to become hectic during the second full week of January and it might occur to you that something you have had planned since before the start of the year is still waiting to be done. You are able to apply yourself to just about anything today and, what is more, it won't bother you if you have to tackle several different tasks.

8 THURSDAY
Moon Age Day 18 Moon Sign Leo

For some Pisceans, there are radical alterations around now and old modes of thinking will be out of the window. Make good use of today, because after this you will be in a much quieter and less progressive frame of mind until Sunday. Friends could prove to be especially useful when it comes to achieving a longed-for objective.

9 FRIDAY
Moon Age Day 19 Moon Sign Virgo

The Moon moves into your opposite zodiac sign of Virgo today, bringing that part of the month known as the lunar low. You are less energetic at this time and more inclined to find a small corner in which you can sit and think. This is no bad thing for Pisces, because it is out of your musing now that success comes later.

10 SATURDAY
Moon Age Day 20 Moon Sign Virgo

Getting involved in interesting new projects will have to wait because if you try too hard at the moment you could find yourself falling at the first hurdle. Let others take some of the strain whilst you cosset yourself a little. You should be back on fine form by tomorrow, but for the moment you will simply have to show some patience.

11 SUNDAY
Moon Age Day 21 Moon Sign Virgo

Any power struggles are likely to come to a head now – simply because you are far less likely to back down in the face of opposition. Certain people are about to discover just how powerful you can be and they are certain to be impressed. At home you show a different face and will be charm itself to those you love.

12 MONDAY
Moon Age Day 22 Moon Sign Libra

The start of the week should find you anxious to carry on making a good impression with relatives and the social side of your nature is also well emphasised. No matter what the winter weather throws at you, there is scope for getting out of the house and doing something different. A shopping spree with friends might well appeal to you.

13 TUESDAY
Moon Age Day 23 Moon Sign Libra

Things tend to go your way in most respects for the moment and you will be actively seeking ways to get ahead, especially in your home life. There are positive ways to show people how much you care and these are not lost on you at the moment. Much of your attention could be focused on practical and financial matters.

14 WEDNESDAY
Moon Age Day 24 Moon Sign Scorpio

The needs and wants of loved ones are inclined to play on your mind today. There is nothing especially surprising about that, because it is the way you often think. However, it is also important to bear your own requirements in mind, because if you are not comfortable yourself you can't be of much use to anyone else.

15 THURSDAY
Moon Age Day 25 Moon Sign Scorpio

A plan of action that you have found fairly exciting of late could prove to be something of a disappointment. If this turns out to be the case, it is essential that you retrench and begin again immediately. Only by constantly applying yourself and by refusing to take no for an answer can you really win through at the moment.

16 FRIDAY
Moon Age Day 26 Moon Sign Scorpio

You seem to be very much in control of things today – and how true this is where personal attachments are concerned. When it comes to romance, you are unquestionably holding the tiller and should find that your level of popularity is on the increase, even with people who don't normally seem to like you. Be definite today in the way you handle money.

17 SATURDAY
Moon Age Day 27 Moon Sign Sagittarius

This may be the best time for business that you have experienced so far in January. You seem automatically to have what it takes to make the right decisions and could be called upon to accept new responsibilities. These may not bring in more money in themselves, but seem to be preparing the way for a better financial phase.

18 SUNDAY
Moon Age Day 28 Moon Sign Sagittarius

There ought to be no shortage of interest around you now and if there is any problem at all today it could be the difficulty of making your mind up what you are going to do when so much is on offer. Keep your eyes open for some interesting new people who are likely to be coming into your life around this time and get to know them.

19 MONDAY
Moon Age Day 29 Moon Sign Capricorn

It looks as though you are going to have significantly more grit and determination at the commencement of this particular week, but you won't get on all that well unless you plan carefully. Too many hasty actions are definitely to be avoided and you will need to show your ingenious side if you are going to make gains across the board.

20 TUESDAY
Moon Age Day 0 Moon Sign Capricorn

The sort of people you definitely get on well with today are those who are funny and who are natural givers. On the other hand, you won't see eye to eye with selfish or sarcastic types. You will also be doing all you can to support the underdog in almost any situation and tend to show your most charitable side at the moment.

21 WEDNESDAY
Moon Age Day 1 Moon Sign Aquarius

Understanding others and being able to premeditate what they are likely to do – and when – can be a distinct advantage to you now. Your attitude to life at the moment is realistic and you tend to work very hard towards your objectives. Not everyone appreciates you, but the most important people certainly will today.

22 THURSDAY   ☿
Moon Age Day 2 Moon Sign Aquarius

Unexpected changes could come along today and that is something you don't take to very well. You might be somewhat nervy and inclined to allow others to take the lead, but in your heart you know what you want to do and you merely have to defer these actions for a short while. Don't make huge commitments until later.

23 FRIDAY   ☿
Moon Age Day 3 Moon Sign Pisces

The end of this new working week also brings a change of attitude in you. The Moon has now moved into your own zodiac sign of Pisces, bringing that part of the month known as the lunar high. Keep your eyes open for Lady Luck, because she is never far from your life under such trends.

24 SATURDAY   ☿
Moon Age Day 4 Moon Sign Pisces

This is a time during which innovative changes are absolutely essential. You want to alter your living or working environment and will have everything you need to do so. Even if certain people seem to be throwing obstacles in your path, you find ways and means to turn difficulties into genuine and long-lasting successes.

25 SUNDAY ☿ *Moon Age Day 5 Moon Sign Aries*

The sort of progress you make today can be smooth and seamless, which suits you down to the ground. Attitude is everything when you are dealing with people who can often be awkward, but you shouldn't make too much allowance for them today. On the contrary, if you are assertive and show them you mean business they will comply.

26 MONDAY ☿ *Moon Age Day 6 Moon Sign Aries*

There is likely to be more than one issue trying your patience at present and it is most important at the start of this particular working week that you keep your cool. The more you take things in your stride, the greater the level of trust you get from others. Some people may be deliberately testing you, so don't react badly.

27 TUESDAY ☿ *Moon Age Day 7 Moon Sign Taurus*

With the Moon in Taurus, you seem to be at your most practical and can get through jobs in half the usual time. It doesn't matter whether you are sorting out something very complicated at work or doing some chores around the house. Everything you undertake is now done logically and in the knowledge that you will succeed.

28 WEDNESDAY ☿ *Moon Age Day 8 Moon Sign Taurus*

You will be happy to spend as much time as possible today with loved ones and won't be all that keen to spread your wings. Maybe that isn't surprising in the middle of the winter, but for whatever reason you will be quite happy to put your feet up and sit in front of a warm fire. Seek out a really good book or enjoy the television.

29 THURSDAY ☿ *Moon Age Day 9 Moon Sign Gemini*

Casual social contacts work best and you are likely to meet some people who haven't figured in your life up until now. Some of these individuals could be quite captivating and they seem to be the sort of people who have done everything you haven't. Listen to their stories, but don't forget you have tales of your own.

30 FRIDAY ☿ *Moon Age Day 10 Moon Sign Gemini*

You now seem to be at your best when practical common sense is required, but at the same time you are also deeply romantic in your thoughts and actions. How could you fail to please your lover when you are so attentive and kind? When you are involved in group activities, you are still less likely to take the lead and will be happy to follow.

31 SATURDAY ☿

Moon Age Day 11 Moon Sign Gemini

Things that happen today bring out the detective in you and make you want to solve all manner of puzzles – not just those that appear in books or newspapers. You are in exactly the right frame of mind to be turning over stones all the time and you won't be at all content when you are faced with a problem unless you know how to solve it.

♓ February
2015

Your Month at a Glance

$\oplus$ = Opportunities are around   ⊖ = Be on the defensive   ● = Life is pretty ordinary

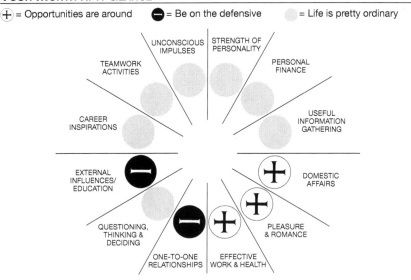

UNCONSCIOUS IMPULSES
STRENGTH OF PERSONALITY
TEAMWORK ACTIVITIES
PERSONAL FINANCE
CAREER INSPIRATIONS
USEFUL INFORMATION GATHERING
EXTERNAL INFLUENCES/ EDUCATION
DOMESTIC AFFAIRS
QUESTIONING, THINKING & DECIDING
PLEASURE & ROMANCE
ONE-TO-ONE RELATIONSHIPS
EFFECTIVE WORK & HEALTH

February Highs and Lows

Here I show you how the rhythms of the Moon will affect you this month. Like the tide, your energies and abilities will rise and fall with its pattern. When it is above the centre line, go for it, when it is below, you should be resting.

HIGH 19TH–20TH

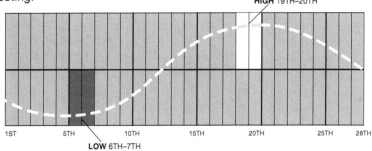

1ST   5TH   10TH   15TH   20TH   25TH   28TH

LOW 6TH–7TH

52

1 SUNDAY ☿ *Moon Age Day 12 Moon Sign Cancer*

It might be necessary to stand up for yourself in some way today. You are not the sort of person to make a fuss unnecessarily, but when the chips are down you simply won't be blamed for something you didn't do. In fact, the sign of Pisces can be quite caustic when necessity arises. Personal relationships should offer enjoyment.

2 MONDAY ☿ *Moon Age Day 13 Moon Sign Cancer*

Standard responses probably won't work at the moment. On the contrary, you need to be original in your thinking and in the things you are saying to others. It is possible to make significant progress in your life at the moment, but you will probably have to pretend to be someone else when a small amount of aggression is called for.

3 TUESDAY ☿ *Moon Age Day 14 Moon Sign Leo*

A little confusion is possible when you are dealing with matters you don't understand very well. The best way forward is to ask someone who does know and you should find his or her responses more than gratifying. All that is happening is people are repaying the some of the many favours they have had from you.

4 WEDNESDAY ☿ *Moon Age Day 15 Moon Sign Leo*

This should be a fairly relaxing day and one during which you have the necessary time to turn your attention towards home and family – always an important consideration as far as you are concerned. The period ahead requires some careful planning, because there are good and bad aspects in the offing.

5 THURSDAY ☿ *Moon Age Day 16 Moon Sign Leo*

Look out for possible changes to your professional life. This may not be quite as bad as it sounds, because it looks as though you may soon be made responsible for something you find distinctly interesting. Someone you don't see too often could be getting in touch, or perhaps you will be phoning or emailing them.

6 FRIDAY ☿ *Moon Age Day 17 Moon Sign Virgo*

There are a couple of days ahead during which you have to exercise a little more care. The lunar low is inclined to bring you face to face with situations you don't care for all that much and life can become distinctly tedious in a number of ways. The best action is to ring the changes when you can, but also to remain patient.

7 SATURDAY ☿ *Moon Age Day 18 Moon Sign Virgo*

Your energy levels are now apt to be quite low and you could do worse than to take some time to yourself. This isn't really a problem for you, because solitary moments can be quite appealing. Don't take on too much. Let people to do things for themselves, rather than running round after them.

8 SUNDAY ☿ *Moon Age Day 19 Moon Sign Libra*

A more active and enterprising day opens up for you and it is one during which you have to take the initiative if you want to get ahead. This should not be too difficult under present trends and it appears that you are quite anxious to show a slightly more aggressive face to the world than normal.

9 MONDAY ☿ *Moon Age Day 20 Moon Sign Libra*

Standard responses sometimes won't work today, so you need to be original in your dealings with others. Attitude is very important when you are approaching new hobbies or pastimes and these must represent something you find personally appealing. Trying to please everyone won't be enough now.

10 TUESDAY ☿ *Moon Age Day 21 Moon Sign Libra*

Refuse to be budged over an issue you see as being very important. Although you could be in for something of a struggle, those around you will gain a new respect for you when you stick up for yourself. Pisces is very chatty at the moment and responds positively to interesting and stimulating conversation.

11 WEDNESDAY ☿ *Moon Age Day 22 Moon Sign Scorpio*

You will probably feel the need to broaden your horizons in some way. Pisces is now starting to be more progressive and forward-looking than has been the case since the start of the year. At the same time you should notice that romantic responses coming at you are much more obvious and you might even have a new admirer.

12 THURSDAY ☿ *Moon Age Day 23 Moon Sign Scorpio*

It is possible that you will feel slightly uncomfortable when you know that others are putting you on some sort of pedestal. This uneasy feeling is understandable but not logical. Have confidence in yourself, because you won't let anyone down and can come up with the goods whenever it proves necessary today.

13 FRIDAY ☿   *Moon Age Day 24 Moon Sign Sagittarius*

You may already have got yourself into a weekend frame of mind, in which case some of the trials and tribulations of your working life won't appeal all that much. Nevertheless, you tend to soldier on because that is the way you are made. By the evening, you need to spread your wings socially.

14 SATURDAY   *Moon Age Day 25 Moon Sign Sagittarius*

Generally positive trends continue but you might not be able to achieve all you would wish with the arrival of the weekend. The answer is simple: don't try. Instead of trying to get ahead in any way, try to enjoy yourself today and tomorrow. Friends should be keen to join in.

15 SUNDAY   *Moon Age Day 26 Moon Sign Capricorn*

Keep up your efforts to get cracking with new projects. You are very sure of yourself just now and this would be the ideal period to push yourself a little. Relatives and friends should be willing to put a shoulder to the wheel if necessary and you probably won't go short of compliments around this time.

16 MONDAY   *Moon Age Day 27 Moon Sign Capricorn*

Part of what you excel at right now is looking after other people. There is nothing in the least unusual about this for a Pisces subject, but you are inclined to be extra attentive at the moment. Almost everyone you meet will respond to your natural kindness and easygoing attitude.

17 TUESDAY   *Moon Age Day 28 Moon Sign Aquarius*

Don't believe everything you hear today, because if you do there is just a chance you could be duped by someone. The best way to avoid this is to use your intuition, which is as strong as that possessed by any zodiac sign. Routines have their own satisfaction now and you keep going when others get bored.

18 WEDNESDAY   *Moon Age Day 29 Moon Sign Aquarius*

Not all of your responses appear to be very practical at the moment, but you can see deep into the heart of situations and will be using some very original ways of sorting things out. Friends warm to your nature and will be more than willing to confide in you – sometimes in ways that could shock you slightly.

19 THURSDAY
Moon Age Day 0 Moon Sign Pisces

There is good company about as the lunar high comes along and this can make all the difference to your own attitude and actions. With good fortune definitely on your side you can afford to take a few chances and few people will miss out on the absolutely charming and yet very dynamic Pisces that is on offer.

20 FRIDAY
Moon Age Day 1 Moon Sign Pisces

Confidence remains high and you will find yourself doing things you have shied away from in the past. Don't hold back, especially when you know something that could be to your own advantage and that of the people you care for. Almost any course of action is legitimate with the Moon in your zodiac sign.

21 SATURDAY
Moon Age Day 2 Moon Sign Aries

Spend at least part of today doing something that just pleases you. So much of your life is given over to helping others that you sometimes fail to address issues that are specifically important to your own life. You will revel in interesting company today and can be the life and soul of social situations.

22 SUNDAY
Moon Age Day 3 Moon Sign Aries

There is no letup in the generally hectic lifestyle you are presently adopting and it is likely that new responsibilities fall upon your shoulders around now. These don't come like a bolt from the blue, but are present because you show yourself to be so capable that others cannot fail to notice.

23 MONDAY
Moon Age Day 4 Moon Sign Aries

Don't force your opinions on to others and avoid appearing to know everything. It isn't often that Pisces comes across as in any way arrogant, but that is the way you could be seen just at the moment. People are so used to your natural humility that an over-confident Pisces individual is a real shocker.

24 TUESDAY
Moon Age Day 5 Moon Sign Taurus

Peace and quiet will probably return for a day or two. This could be a slight problem because those around you have monitored just how go-getting you were yesterday. In most situations you will be more than happy to take a backseat and you won't be inclined to push your ideas on to others.

25 WEDNESDAY
Moon Age Day 6 Moon Sign Taurus

Along comes a period of much stronger personal magnetism – so much so that your romantic life should be much more interesting. Friends should be warm and very attentive and you are likely to be feeling as contented as has been the case since the very start of this year.

26 THURSDAY
Moon Age Day 7 Moon Sign Gemini

You won't be getting on well with everyone and could tend to react quite strongly if you think that you personally or someone to whom you are attached is being victimised. Those on the receiving end of your wrath could be very surprised, because it isn't like you to go off the deep end very often.

27 FRIDAY
Moon Age Day 8 Moon Sign Gemini

Social groups and co-operative matters are now right up your street. You get together with others and can sort out situations that have been either irritating or a puzzle for quite some time. Your mind also turns towards the plight of those who are much less well off and you will want to help all you can.

28 SATURDAY
Moon Age Day 9 Moon Sign Cancer

The trends for the weekend are definitely mixed and you tend to split your time between social occasions and the requirements of home. What really shines out at the moment is your sincerity and there isn't any doubt that people will trust you now with their innermost secrets.

2015

Your Month at a Glance

⊕ = Opportunities are around   ⊖ = Be on the defensive   ⚪ = Life is pretty ordinary

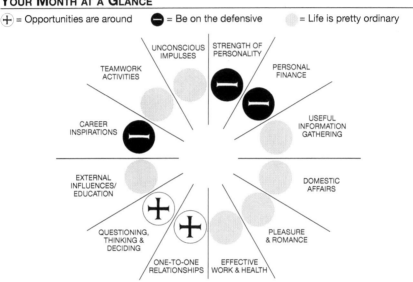

March Highs and Lows

Here I show you how the rhythms of the Moon will affect you this month. Like the tide, your energies and abilities will rise and fall with its pattern. When it is above the centre line, go for it, when it is below, you should be resting.

HIGH 19TH–20TH

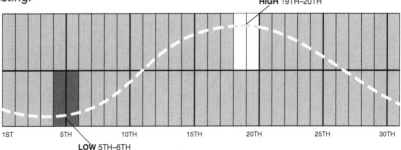

LOW 5TH–6TH

1 SUNDAY
Moon Age Day 10 Moon Sign Cancer

You will be doing your best to please others at the moment and should have little difficulty proving just how conscientious and caring you are. It would be wise to take some time over important jobs, because you might take on more than you can realistically handle.

2 MONDAY
Moon Age Day 11 Moon Sign Leo

Your positive outlook tends to make you quite popular today and you will be especially successful when with groups of people. Your social conscience could easily be aroused by events that happen in your locality and, as is usually the case for Pisces, you will be doing what you can to help others.

3 TUESDAY
Moon Age Day 12 Moon Sign Leo

Although you tend to be somewhat more thoughtful today, this is no bad thing. Present trends show you to be mulling things over more, but the conclusions you reach are far from being theoretical and have genuine practical value. Standing up for the rights of others will not be far from your mind at any time this month.

4 WEDNESDAY
Moon Age Day 13 Moon Sign Leo

You seem to be in the mood for planning – maybe for a journey that will come a little further down the line. Co-operation with family members is apt to be good and there could be a lot of happiness about at the moment. Try for something different today, because you won't feel like committing yourself to too many routines.

5 THURSDAY
Moon Age Day 14 Moon Sign Virgo

Things should slow somewhat as the lunar low comes around again. This day would be better for planning than doing and you could find those around you slightly more difficult to deal with than has been the case recently. Try to maintain an optimistic attitude, even when things go wrong.

6 FRIDAY
Moon Age Day 15 Moon Sign Virgo

This is no time to be pushing your luck. Gambling is out at present and you do best when you stick to tasks you both like and understand. Be prepared to follow the lead of others, and when you have the chance use their knowledge and common sense in order to leapfrog a potentially difficult situation.

7 SATURDAY
Moon Age Day 16 Moon Sign Libra

Intimate family relationships are the ones that please you most today, together with romantic attachments that also look particularly good. Conversations are unlikely to be about matters of earth-shattering importance, but even small talk has its place in your life right now.

8 SUNDAY
Moon Age Day 17 Moon Sign Libra

You need to push ahead as much as possible right now, even if this proves to be rather difficult on a Sunday. Plan now for what you want to achieve in a practical sense in the days ahead and enlist the help and support of family members. Pisces is very tidy-minded under present trends, so you will hate clutter.

9 MONDAY
Moon Age Day 18 Moon Sign Libra

This may be one of the best days of the month for pleasant relationships and for turning social advantages into business opportunities. Just about everyone you meet today seems to have something good to say to and about you. All the compliments are certain to boost your ego and that can only be a positive thing.

10 TUESDAY
Moon Age Day 19 Moon Sign Scorpio

What matters most now is a positive outlook and with support coming from a number of different astrological directions it seems as though you have what it takes to make significant ground in your life generally. Romance appears to be blossoming, too, even if you have to give it a little nudge.

11 WEDNESDAY
Moon Age Day 20 Moon Sign Scorpio

Today is good for practical developments, even if there are few irritating delays to be dealt with. You have gained some pace during the last couple of days and so you won't take kindly to being stopped in your tracks. It seems as though people will still have to move aside for the steamroller you have become.

12 THURSDAY
Moon Age Day 21 Moon Sign Sagittarius

Information comes in from every conceivable direction at the moment and simply keeping up with the pace of life can be difficult enough. It would be best to stick to an ordered routine if you want to get everything done, but it is unlikely that life itself will offer you that opportunity. As a result you must think on your feet.

13 FRIDAY
Moon Age Day 22 Moon Sign Sagittarius

Problems must be attacked, because the more issues you put on the shelf today, the greater will be your need to deal with all of them at once tomorrow. You have what it takes to be definite, decisive and assertive. There are certain situations in which others won't like this Piscean, but that's just too bad for them.

14 SATURDAY
Moon Age Day 23 Moon Sign Sagittarius

Self-belief is sometimes a problem for Pisces, but that doesn't appear to be the case at the moment. On the contrary, you know what you are good at and tend to stick to that when circumstances allow. You should even be quite bold and assertive in social situations, which could surprise one or two people.

15 SUNDAY
Moon Age Day 24 Moon Sign Capricorn

Your natural warmth is a joy to others and you simply cannot help being liked. This should mean you receive a great deal of positive attention during Sunday and you might have to run to catch up with all the possibilities that are on offer. You can solve a particular problem by breaking it down into its component parts.

16 MONDAY
Moon Age Day 25 Moon Sign Capricorn

You can focus now on getting work developments into a good shape, because it looks as though you are very efficient at the moment. A little more ambition goes a long way and you are now more likely to push for your objectives, rather than waiting until fortune seems to favour you.

17 TUESDAY
Moon Age Day 26 Moon Sign Aquarius

Positive interactions with those in a position of authority get you noticed and you are seeking new horizons wherever possible. Use this positive phase to get what you want, not just for yourself but also on account of those you care for. Don't be too quick to take offence over a statement that sounds rather too personal.

18 WEDNESDAY
Moon Age Day 27 Moon Sign Aquarius

Don't be put off by those who seem incapable of following a simple instruction. The best way forward today is to do most things yourself; at least that way you can be fairly certain they will be done. Take some time out to smell the spring air and to register the changing nature of the seasons.

19 THURSDAY
Moon Age Day 28 Moon Sign Pisces

All of a sudden your mind works very differently and there could hardly be better trends for this stage of the working week than those that surround you now. The lunar high gives you all the incentive you could possibly need to get ahead and every advantage now looks as big as a bus from your perspective.

20 FRIDAY
Moon Age Day 0 Moon Sign Pisces

You now need to be pushing ahead with all guns blazing. What you do today can have a great bearing on both the short and long-term future and since you are competent, forward-looking and even somewhat aggressive, the world won't stand in your way. Refuse to be beaten because you can break your own records right now.

21 SATURDAY
Moon Age Day 1 Moon Sign Aries

Teamwork is good for you under present trends and although you might not be committed to work on a Saturday there are things that need doing and all group activities are favoured. Don't sit around waiting for things to happen. This is an interlude that depends almost entirely on your own efforts.

22 SUNDAY
Moon Age Day 2 Moon Sign Aries

This is an excellent time to be taking on large, ambitious projects. Look for the real joy in your life, because it is just around the next corner. You show a great response to others and will be able to lighten the load of just about anyone. Activity is certainly your thing now and you give all you can to the world at large.

23 MONDAY
Moon Age Day 3 Moon Sign Taurus

Work matters continue to be very productive and you can benefit from taking on new tasks and looking at existing situations in a different way. There isn't quite the level of good luck you have been experiencing across the last few days, but that won't matter too much because you are making your own luck as you go along.

24 TUESDAY
Moon Age Day 4 Moon Sign Taurus

Monetary prospects look fairly good now and this might be an opportune time to consider some sort of limited speculation. People you haven't seen for ages could be making another show in your life and you will also be in touch with people who live at a distance. Get some fresh air and a change of scene at some stage today.

25 WEDNESDAY
Moon Age Day 5 Moon Sign Gemini

Things will steady down somewhat, but that might be no bad thing. You have been on the go solidly for days and would respond well to a period during which you can think about things more fully. Don't get involved in family rows or fall out with friends over situations that really aren't worth the bother.

26 THURSDAY
Moon Age Day 6 Moon Sign Gemini

There is good news coming along today, but you may need to keep your ears open if you are not to miss a very real opportunity to shine. Love is uppermost in your mind, more so than at any time so far this month. True to your zodiac sign, you are caring and show every desire to share what you have.

27 FRIDAY
Moon Age Day 7 Moon Sign Cancer

You remain fairly optimistic and quite willing to do whatever is necessary to impress others and to get what you most want from life. Although not a particularly inspiring sort of day, this is a solid time and a period during which you can consolidate efforts that you have been putting in for a while.

28 SATURDAY
Moon Age Day 8 Moon Sign Cancer

Get what you want by being willing to ask for it. A little cheek can go a long way and you are able to provide yourself with extra security in your life when it matters the most. Much of your attention at the moment is being given to domestic issues and the wellbeing of your nearest and dearest.

29 SUNDAY
Moon Age Day 9 Moon Sign Cancer

You can make progress if you are able to channel personal energies properly. The only slight difficulty is that you may be more easily confused by different options today. It would be good to make up your mind quickly and once you have settled on a course of action make sure you pursue it fully.

30 MONDAY
Moon Age Day 10 Moon Sign Leo

Concentrate for the moment on firming up personal securities and do everything you can to get on side with people who seem to have a great deal of influence. You might choose to take the odd chance financially and as long as you genuinely do have one eye on the future you are unlikely to go wrong.

31 TUESDAY
Moon Age Day 11   Moon Sign Leo

Your successes are often quiet and more considered and you move forward after due thought. Those around you may now think you are acting in a way that is typical of your usual nature. All the same, you retain a burning desire to get on well and will still be putting effort into potential future projects.

2015

Your Month at a Glance

⊕ = Opportunities are around   ⊖ = Be on the defensive   ⬤ = Life is pretty ordinary

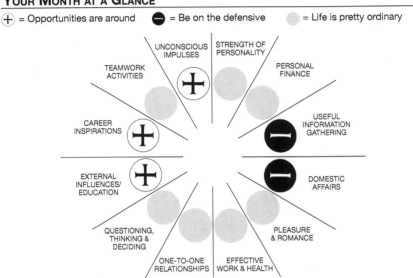

April Highs and Lows

Here I show you how the rhythms of the Moon will affect you this month. Like the tide, your energies and abilities will rise and fall with its pattern. When it is above the centre line, go for it, when it is below, you should be resting.

HIGH 15TH–16TH

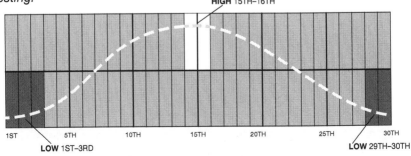

1ST   5TH   10TH   15TH   20TH   25TH   30TH

LOW 1ST–3RD   **LOW** 29TH–30TH

1 WEDNESDAY
Moon Age Day 12 Moon Sign Virgo

You may experience setbacks at this time, mainly due to the appearance of the lunar low. If you feel slightly down in the dumps, console yourself with the thought that this is only a short period and one that won't have any bearing on the general trends of life. This is likely to be quieter than the average day.

2 THURSDAY
Moon Age Day 13 Moon Sign Virgo

A developing tendency towards daydreaming is going to become obvious as today advances. There is nothing at all wrong with this, just as long as you keep at least one foot in the real world. Once the cares of the day are out of the way, you might decide to disappear into the pages of a really good book.

3 FRIDAY
Moon Age Day 14 Moon Sign Virgo

The current lunar low is unlikely to have too much of an impact on your life, because there are so many planetary influences that support you at the moment. All the same, it would be better to avoid taking chances today and gambling is certainly out. Listen to what a friend is trying to tell you.

4 SATURDAY
Moon Age Day 15 Moon Sign Libra

Communication issues make life look especially interesting at present. You may not always understand what those around you are talking about, but you do have what it takes to bluff your way through certain situations. Once you have time to reflect, everything should become clearer.

5 SUNDAY
Moon Age Day 16 Moon Sign Libra

There could be a little more in the way of pessimism about today, probably because you are expected to do something that takes more confidence than you think you possess. It's time to take your courage in both your hands and to push forward. Everything should turn out right in the end.

6 MONDAY
Moon Age Day 17 Moon Sign Scorpio

Beware of a little sentimentality creeping in today, because it will take the edge off your natural abilities and prevent you from making the sort of progress you most need right now. The Piscean mind is apt to look to the past quite frequently, but there is little help there for you at this time.

7 TUESDAY
Moon Age Day 18 Moon Sign Scorpio

Don't just look at problems, but rather attack them as early in the day as you can. That will leave you the time you need to do what pleases you. Pisces now needs luxury in its life, even if this is sometimes sacrificed for the needs of others. Treat yourself a little and allow those around you to spoil you, because you deserve it.

8 WEDNESDAY
Moon Age Day 19 Moon Sign Scorpio

You want to look forward, especially in a professional sense, but there are a great many variables to bear in mind. It would be better to let things ride for a day or two, whilst you concentrate on making yourself more comfortable in a general sense. As always, you register the kindness of those around you.

9 THURSDAY
Moon Age Day 20 Moon Sign Sagittarius

You may feel that home is the best place to be right now, possibly because something in the outside world feels slightly threatening. What a great time this would be for a reunion of some sort or for getting in touch with people who for one reason or another you haven't seen recently.

10 FRIDAY
Moon Age Day 21 Moon Sign Sagittarius

There could be some very favourable times coming along in terms of your romantic life and you are in the right frame of mind to respond positively to these. Since your popularity is high at present it is also possible that compliments will come in from some fairly unexpected directions. Try to take these in your stride.

11 SATURDAY
Moon Age Day 22 Moon Sign Capricorn

You might think it apt to turn towards short-term goals now, at least partly because you want to see things getting done. New starts are quite possible and you won't have quite as much patience as usual, especially with individuals who jump about from one foot to the other.

12 SUNDAY
Moon Age Day 23 Moon Sign Capricorn

Try not to be too impulsive today or it could lead to misunderstandings. It is good to do things your own way, but the odd explanation would help. This weekend, you need to be doing something that takes you completely out of yourself. Keep in touch with friends and maybe arrange to see them today.

13 MONDAY
Moon Age Day 24 Moon Sign Aquarius

At the start of a new working week, you will have plenty of energy to pour into your job. Pisces is extremely capable at this time and the support of the planet Mars in particular makes you more decisive and possibly also slightly more touchy than normal.

14 TUESDAY
Moon Age Day 25 Moon Sign Aquarius

Personalities tend to crop up all the time today and you should find a good deal of enjoyment from simply being in their company. Yours tends to be more of a supportive role now than has been the case in recent days and you will be happy enough to stand just one step out of the limelight for the moment.

15 WEDNESDAY
Moon Age Day 26 Moon Sign Pisces

The Moon races into the sign of Pisces, where it smiles on you for the next couple of days. That is indeed fortunate for you and the lunar high finds you at your most positive and go-getting. You will still be in the mood for getting away from routines, but now you are also more adventurous.

16 THURSDAY
Moon Age Day 27 Moon Sign Pisces

You can make a very positive impression on this part of the week. If you are in a position of some authority at work, this is a period during which the attention of superiors is focused on you. As a rule this might make you very nervous, but the lunar high allows you to take almost anything in your stride.

17 FRIDAY
Moon Age Day 28 Moon Sign Aries

If you discover a personal issue that has been left up in the air, this is the time to sort it out. Keeping things to yourself is certainly not the answer and you need to keep talking today if you expect others to know the way you feel. Find the time for a good old chat with someone you care for.

18 SATURDAY
Moon Age Day 29 Moon Sign Aries

All matters to do with communication should be positively highlighted under present trends and you won't want to be spending too much time on your own. There is a hint of wanderlust about you at present and if you have the chance to see over the next horizon then so much the better.

19 SUNDAY
Moon Age Day 0 Moon Sign Taurus

This is a really good time for you as far as domestic circumstances are concerned. You are able to persuade family members to follow your lead and young people especially seem easier to deal with. Most of the projects you take on around this time are likely to be associated with your home in some way.

20 MONDAY
Moon Age Day 1 Moon Sign Taurus

Not everything that happens today will seem to be in your best interest, but you can turn situations round if you think carefully. You need to proceed with just a little caution and to take some of the things that people tell you with a pinch of salt. Romance should be looking good for many Pisceans.

21 TUESDAY
Moon Age Day 2 Moon Sign Gemini

You may not be able to get ahead at the moment without taking risks, but these are going to be very calculated ones and are only undertaken after great thought. Your schedule is likely to be quite full at this time and there won't be as much time as usual for small talk and for chatting to friends.

22 WEDNESDAY
Moon Age Day 3 Moon Sign Gemini

You should be able to have more time to yourself now and will relish those quiet moments during which you can think about life and organise yourself for later. Something at the back of your mind will probably be telling you that this is a time for spring-cleaning and there is real action on the way.

23 THURSDAY
Moon Age Day 4 Moon Sign Gemini

Your thoughts are uplifted by a generally optimistic attitude that seems to permeate every aspect of life. Get in gear as soon as you can today and make the most of every small opportunity that comes your way. People are likely to be kind and considerate – in fact, they treat you as you treat them.

24 FRIDAY
Moon Age Day 5 Moon Sign Cancer

This is a good time to be around others in a social sense and romantic contacts are well starred under present astrological trends. Who knows, you might even discover you have an unexpected admirer, and you are certainly top of the list when it comes to invitations.

25 SATURDAY
Moon Age Day 6   Moon Sign Cancer

It looks as though you are gradually becoming more acquisitive on the one hand and yet tidier, too. This means that when you get something new at the moment you may feel obliged to ditch something that is no longer of use to you. Actually making up your mind to throw anything away could be more difficult than you expect.

26 SUNDAY
Moon Age Day 7   Moon Sign Leo

When it comes to major decisions you need to take your time, but you can't wait around too long jumping from foot to foot. Once you are sure that your intended action is the best possible, get cracking. Friends could be taxing your patience, but being a Pisces you have plenty of that commodity.

27 MONDAY
Moon Age Day 8   Moon Sign Leo

Life remains generally busy, yet at the same time you have a yearning for something more. Plan now for holidays and if it proves to be possible, get yourself out and about in the very near future. You may long to know what lies over the next horizon and the only real way to be sure is to go and take a look.

28 TUESDAY
Moon Age Day 9   Moon Sign Leo

There will be no time for rehearsals today. You need to be quick in your thinking and very positive in your responses. Don't get tied up in red tape and make certain that all your actions are for a purpose. By the end of the day you may be slowing down somewhat, probably because you have exhausted yourself.

29 WEDNESDAY
Moon Age Day 10   Moon Sign Virgo

Things should be looking up from a romantic point of view and the middle of the week is also likely to bring more in the way of popularity. It might be quite surprising to find you are flavour of the month with someone who doesn't usually seem to look your way, but make the most of the situation.

30 THURSDAY
Moon Age Day 11   Moon Sign Virgo

Today you are fully future-oriented and committed to making things work out positively, especially at work. Your insights are very good and your intuition is also working very strongly. Advice comes thick and fast from all directions but only a proportion of it is worth following so be discriminating.

May

2015

Your Month at a Glance

(+) = Opportunities are around   ⊖ = Be on the defensive   ● = Life is pretty ordinary

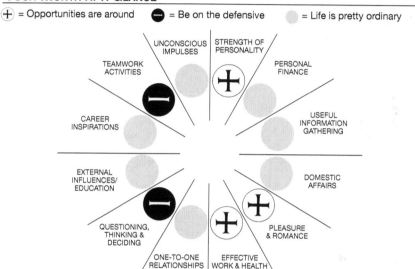

May Highs and Lows

Here I show you how the rhythms of the Moon will affect you this month. Like the tide, your energies and abilities will rise and fall with its pattern. When it is above the centre line, go for it, when it is below, you should be resting.

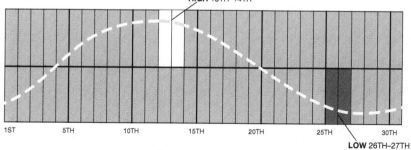

1 FRIDAY
Moon Age Day 12 Moon Sign Libra

Things should generally be back to normal as the Moon moves into Libra. However, normal is a relative term, because there are other planets around at present that increase your intuition to the point at which others may call you a little spooky. Nobody is going to pull the wool over your eyes right now.

2 SATURDAY
Moon Age Day 13 Moon Sign Libra

A slight increase in the pressure you feel being placed upon you can be accommodated easily, even if you panic at first. Get yourself sorted out before you tackle anything new – and this is especially important if you find that you will have to address a number of people. Public speaking isn't usually your thing.

3 SUNDAY
Moon Age Day 14 Moon Sign Libra

It would be best to avoid arguments today, although this might be easier said than done as far as family members are concerned. It appears there is someone close to you who has to question everything you say and do. If you can avoid rising to the bait, so much the better, because there is little to gain from responding.

4 MONDAY
Moon Age Day 15 Moon Sign Scorpio

Make yourself generally useful today and be where things are happening. You won't help your cause by sitting in a corner on your own and simply getting on with things. Present trends show that the more you advertise your presence, the greater the chance that your point of view will be taken on board.

5 TUESDAY
Moon Age Day 16 Moon Sign Scorpio

It looks as though your domestic life is becoming as good as it gets and at least part of this is down to your own attitude. Where there has been some sort of discord, you are the one who will put things right. Even if you have had no direct involvement in such situations you end up being the peacemaker.

6 WEDNESDAY
Moon Age Day 17 Moon Sign Sagittarius

There are new interests on the horizon, some of which are going to take you to places you haven't been before, both inside and outside your head. The more unusual of your qualities are now on display and you will prove to be curious and fascinating to others. Pisces people can be deep and unfathomable pools!

7 THURSDAY
Moon Age Day 18 Moon Sign Sagittarius

Once again that insatiable curiosity wins out, as it will at any time this month that things quieten down a little. You want to know how everything works and there is great intellectual stimulation at every turn. A break from routine would probably be good, even though you might have to leave something until later as a result.

8 FRIDAY
Moon Age Day 19 Moon Sign Capricorn

You never know when situations are going to turn your way and that is especially the case at the moment. Keep your eyes open, because there are ways in which you can push ahead and get something you have wanted for ages. Personal attachments look particularly good and you warm to the overtures of a specific individual.

9 SATURDAY
Moon Age Day 20 Moon Sign Capricorn

You might be quite amazed to discover just how popular you are today and all because you simply do what seems to be the right thing. People will turn to you for advice, and even when you don't really understand the problem you are capable of solving it. It's heart-warming to feel so needed.

10 SUNDAY
Moon Age Day 21 Moon Sign Aquarius

You should have everything you need to move forward in a practical sense and the only thing that appears to be missing is your own motivation. This might be a pointer that something is wrong and that you are not finding the challenges you need the most. Look at life again and do some rearranging.

11 MONDAY
Moon Age Day 22 Moon Sign Aquarius

Avoid the sort of mistakes that come from failing to pay enough attention to what you are doing. Concentration is now very important, especially when you are dealing with subject matter you don't understand very well. Some romantic advantages could be on the way by this evening.

12 TUESDAY
Moon Age Day 23 Moon Sign Aquarius

There could be a new love interest on the horizon for some Pisceans at the moment and for most of you it will be relationships that fill your mind to a significant level. That won't prevent you from doing what is expected of you in a practical sense, because you are efficient and cheerful in your work.

13 WEDNESDAY
Moon Age Day 24   Moon Sign Pisces

You might have been slightly thwarted in your wishes and intentions yesterday because of the lack of opportunities around, but the same cannot be said of today. Push ahead with your plans and don't take no for an answer. You should find that finances are stronger and that you notice a strong element of good luck.

14 THURSDAY
Moon Age Day 25   Moon Sign Pisces

Any tendency towards introspection is now clearly out of the window. The lunar high is present and puts you firmly in the driving seat. Don't be tardy about making up your mind in any situation and let the world know that you are ready to take command. New and better responsibilities could be the result.

15 FRIDAY
Moon Age Day 26   Moon Sign Aries

You benefit today from any sort of extrovert activity and from being involved in physical work of some sort. As far as your intellect is concerned, there is little or nothing that goes over your head. Ordinary rules and regulations may prove to be somewhat annoying, especially if they stop you in your tracks.

16 SATURDAY
Moon Age Day 27   Moon Sign Aries

It's clear that you are now in the mood for excitement and in fact you can find it almost anywhere you go. Friends prove to be quite stimulating in their ideas and suggestions, whilst you might also discover hidden depths within almost anyone. Don't get too hung up on doing the right thing today, and instead simply be yourself.

17 SUNDAY
Moon Age Day 28   Moon Sign Taurus

Not everything that happens today is going to be strictly expected and you will have to react quickly if you want to make profit from instant opportunities. Nobody is in a better position to do this than you and there are strong planetary influences that indicate gains that come about as a result of the intervention of your friends.

18 MONDAY
Moon Age Day 0   Moon Sign Taurus

Pisces now displays a real desire to break out of restrictive situations and with the advancing summer you will also be anxious to spend more time outside. All in all, this would be a fine time to think about a holiday planned at short notice or even a weekend away. Everyday routines can certainly seem quite tedious.

19 TUESDAY ☿ *Moon Age Day 1 Moon Sign Gemini*

You will still be very keen to break out of long-established patterns, even though these can be quite comfortable on occasions. Any feelings of uneasiness are quite understandable, because you rely heavily on the past and also on certain conventions. All the same, change is necessary and, once undertaken, it benefits you.

20 WEDNESDAY ☿ *Moon Age Day 2 Moon Sign Gemini*

Ingenious ideas are there for the taking and all it requires is a little extra effort and courage from you in order to embrace them. Friends in particular have things to say that will spark your imagination and start you thinking down different paths. This is likely to be a period that offers more in the way of excitement.

21 THURSDAY ☿ *Moon Age Day 3 Moon Sign Cancer*

There are people around at the moment who have everything it takes to irritate you. Most likely, there will be little surprise about exactly who is getting your goat, but you do now have what it takes to deal with them in a different way. What matters most is achieving compromises without giving away what is really important to you.

22 FRIDAY ☿ *Moon Age Day 4 Moon Sign Cancer*

You may need to take time out in order to address a few practical issues, while at the same time getting on with the sort of jobs you would prefer to leave alone completely. Who knows? It might be possible to get others to lend a hand, thus turning some irritating chores into a feast of fun. All you really have to do is ask.

23 SATURDAY ☿ *Moon Age Day 5 Moon Sign Leo*

You can expect a few ups and downs within personal relationships this weekend, which is why the wisest amongst you will be spending at least some of your spare time with friends. It might seem especially good to be with people whose emotional attachment to you is not quite so deep and who want to be casual in their approach.

24 SUNDAY ☿ *Moon Age Day 6 Moon Sign Leo*

Using little else but your natural charm, you can get almost anything you want today. It's true that your requirements of life are more modest than most, but even you might decide that you deserve a little more right now. If there are any difficulties within personal and romantic attachments you need to talk things through carefully.

25 MONDAY ☿ *Moon Age Day 7 Moon Sign Leo*

Your personal involvement with co-workers is going to be quite crucial at the beginning of this week, probably because they have something you need, whilst you possess knowledge that is crucial to them. Successful partnerships could be the result, even if these only last a short time. There are some strange alliances to be formed.

26 TUESDAY ☿ *Moon Age Day 8 Moon Sign Virgo*

Be prepared to take practical advice if it is offered today, because chances are you will need it. The lunar low is around and although you find alternatives to some of your plans that go slightly amiss, there are other situations that can only be sorted out with the help of others. Don't try to achieve anything major today.

27 WEDNESDAY ☿ *Moon Age Day 9 Moon Sign Virgo*

You still need a gentle touch on the tiller of life and can probably find the greatest gains today when you are doing nothing in particular. Allow others to take the strain, which will give you a rest and show your confidence in them. Family matters may well be uppermost in your mind.

28 THURSDAY ☿ *Moon Age Day 10 Moon Sign Libra*

Things should get noticeably better as today wears on, and by the evening you might wonder why you were anxious about anything. The pace of life is going to get very fast as this month comes to its end and it would be useful to have a more concrete game plan before you embark on anything particularly adventurous or slightly risky.

29 FRIDAY ☿ *Moon Age Day 11 Moon Sign Libra*

It might be necessary to show a slightly more selfish attitude today. There are times when even Pisces must think of number one, not only for your own sake, but also so that you can be of more use to others later. If you think about things in this way, you won't have half so much guilt when you take time to make things better in your own life.

30 SATURDAY ☿ *Moon Age Day 12 Moon Sign Libra*

Do what you can to improve your lot socially – maybe by mixing with a slightly different set of people and by showing your potential more than you sometimes do. All you really have to do is to turn your charisma up a notch and then wait for the reaction. There isn't much doubt about your ability to influence people around now.

31 SUNDAY ☿

Moon Age Day 13 Moon Sign Scorpio

This might be a very good time to revitalise certain elements of your personal life and to find out exactly what your partner or sweetheart feels about life in general. In most respects you already know, because you are a sensitive soul and always bear others in mind. However, there may be some things that people haven't been telling you.

June

2015

YOUR MONTH AT A GLANCE

(+) = Opportunities are around ⬤ = Be on the defensive ⬤ = Life is pretty ordinary

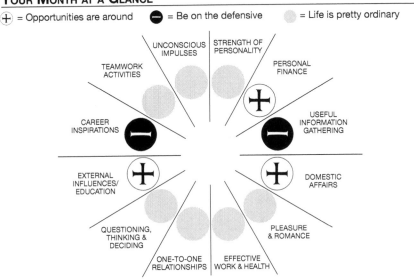

STRENGTH OF PERSONALITY

UNCONSCIOUS IMPULSES

TEAMWORK ACTIVITIES

PERSONAL FINANCE

CAREER INSPIRATIONS

USEFUL INFORMATION GATHERING

EXTERNAL INFLUENCES/ EDUCATION

DOMESTIC AFFAIRS

QUESTIONING, THINKING & DECIDING

PLEASURE & ROMANCE

ONE-TO-ONE RELATIONSHIPS

EFFECTIVE WORK & HEALTH

JUNE HIGHS AND LOWS

Here I show you how the rhythms of the Moon will affect you this month. Like the tide, your energies and abilities will rise and fall with its pattern. When it is above the centre line, go for it, when it is below, you should be resting.

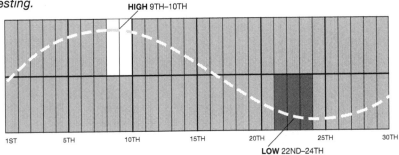

HIGH 9TH–10TH

1ST   5TH   10TH   15TH   20TH   25TH   30TH

LOW 22ND–24TH

I MONDAY *Moon Age Day 14 Moon Sign Scorpio*

There are plenty of different options about today, so don't accept what you know to be second best. Instead of just taking what people are offering, push them to make greater concessions. This is especially true if you are out shopping, because there are some real bargains to had if you are willing to do a little haggling.

2 TUESDAY *Moon Age Day 15 Moon Sign Sagittarius*

Love and social life look to be on a definite roll at the moment. You still show a tendency to smoulder emotionally and that proves to be very attractive to would-be admirers, but you are also extremely funny at present, which others find attractive. Even the odd mistake you make right now can be turned to your advantage.

3 WEDNESDAY *Moon Age Day 16 Moon Sign Sagittarius*

It doesn't take much in the way of effort for you to find yourself in the midst of potentially exciting and very enjoyable situations at present. If anything, you might be having too much fun and could decide by the end of the day that it would be just as much fun to slump down in your favourite chair and rest for a while.

4 THURSDAY *Moon Age Day 17 Moon Sign Sagittarius*

There could be a few difficulties about today and these are be inspired by people who seem determined to be awkward. Rather than wasting your time arguing with such individuals, it would be far better simply to do your own thing and ignore contrary advice. Socially speaking, the day has its ups and downs, but should be reasonable.

5 FRIDAY *Moon Age Day 18 Moon Sign Capricorn*

Whilst you are likely to be on top form as far as communication issues are concerned, you should avoid getting involved in needless competitions with others, simply for the sake of the exercise. Instead you need to work towards your own objectives, whether or not the consensus is on your side. You can win out in the end.

6 SATURDAY *Moon Age Day 19 Moon Sign Capricorn*

In the short term, it might be sensible to make a list of things that need to be done and to approach them in the order of their importance. However, a part of your mind is likely to be focused on the future and it is just as important to have a few moments – or even an hour or two – to sit somewhere quiet and contemplate your intended actions.

7 SUNDAY ☿   *Moon Age Day 20 Moon Sign Aquarius*

It is very rare that Pisces proves to be insensitive to the needs and wants of others, but this might be the case right now. It's not that you are being selfish (a word that doesn't really occur in your vocabulary); it's just that you can't satisfy your own needs right now and also please the world at large.

8 MONDAY ☿   *Moon Age Day 21 Moon Sign Aquarius*

Getting along with specific individuals could be more complicated today, mainly because of the way you are feeling yourself. Don't be too quick to show a critical face to the world, but accept that you can be wrong on occasions. A high-handed attitude won't help at all and might even get you into something of a fix.

9 TUESDAY ☿   *Moon Age Day 22 Moon Sign Pisces*

This could turn out to be the most positive and dynamic lunar high so far this year. This is because the position of the Moon in your sign of Pisces is backed up by a whole host of other positive planetary positions. Make the most of today by being willing to have a go at anything and do all you can to attract others.

10 WEDNESDAY ☿   *Moon Age Day 23 Moon Sign Pisces*

You continue to act and think in a very positive way and can expect to get a very good reaction from others as a result. Those people who come into your life around this time could prove to be of tremendous use to you both now and in the near future. In particular, you are keen to emphasise and enjoy your social life.

11 THURSDAY ☿   *Moon Age Day 24 Moon Sign Aries*

You are very business-minded, but will be more inclined to go for the safe option today. As long as you speak out for yourself this won't be a problem, because it means that people can see both sides of your nature. When it comes to your personal life, there will be far less inhibition and Pisces remains showy, sexy and powerful.

12 FRIDAY ☿   *Moon Age Day 25 Moon Sign Aries*

Getting fellow workers on your side – or even friends – is going to be quite easy now and your ability to co-operate is about as good as it gets. Pisces is sometimes a definite loner, but not at the moment. It is the stimulus you get from others that offers you the really good ideas that will brighten your life no end today.

13 SATURDAY
Moon Age Day 26 Moon Sign Taurus

A little speculation might work well today, though you do need to be careful that you don't invest everything you have in one scheme that looks somewhat risky. Rather, you need to spread your efforts in a number of different directions and then you may well benefit from them all. Avoid any sort of pretence when dealing with your partner.

14 SUNDAY
Moon Age Day 27 Moon Sign Taurus

Changes to your financial situation could begin to offer you more in the way of security and a greater sense of being in charge of your own destiny. This in turn can lead to greater comfort in your surroundings, because you may decide that you can afford to splash out on something that is entirely for the sake of luxury.

15 MONDAY
Moon Age Day 28 Moon Sign Gemini

You can now take decisive action to improve your personal finances and will also be laying down plans that should see you better off in the longer-term future too. Pisces is very courageous at the moment and will stop at nothing to pursue a dream. Romantic overtures are on the way, even if you don't expect them at all.

16 TUESDAY
Moon Age Day 29 Moon Sign Gemini

Despite having mainly positive social influences surrounding you at present, you might be slightly less engaging than usual. This is because you are keeping yourself busy and because you recognise that there are certain things that simply have to be done. Try to split your time between various activities, if you can.

17 WEDNESDAY
Moon Age Day 0 Moon Sign Cancer

You remain less inclined to mix freely with others and will probably indulge in solo activities or ones that commit you to specific individuals whom you know very well. This is a time during which you are thinking deeply and probably planning strategies for the medium and long-term future.

18 THURSDAY
Moon Age Day 1 Moon Sign Cancer

Relationships now prove to be very empowering and it is thanks to your association with others that you make significant headway at the moment. Almost anyone can help you along, even strangers. Mixing with groups or associations of people would also seem to be a sensible strategy now.

19 FRIDAY
Moon Age Day 2 Moon Sign Cancer

Pisces is now likely to be more assertive than usual and somewhat outspoken. At the same time, with Mars in its present position you will be putting a great deal of energy into matters that have to do with your family or the place where you live. You need to feel comfortable now for maximum success.

20 SATURDAY
Moon Age Day 3 Moon Sign Leo

You have the ability to command attention and to get others to do your bidding. This is not achieved by bullying, but rather by a mixture of compliments and positive suggestions. Don't be in the least surprised if you find yourself deluged by text messages, emails and letters at the moment.

21 SUNDAY
Moon Age Day 4 Moon Sign Leo

Pisces now shows its more passionate side. This will probably be restricted to personal attachments, because you are unlikely to be expressing your deepest longings to the world at large. You have the right words within you at the moment to sweep someone off their feet.

22 MONDAY
Moon Age Day 5 Moon Sign Virgo

There is just a chance that you might fail to see the really important issues at the moment, mainly because you are dealing with so many routine chores. There are moments today when you need to surface from the dross and to see the sky shining above your head. Make a conscious decision to take an hour to yourself.

23 TUESDAY
Moon Age Day 6 Moon Sign Virgo

If yesterday was somewhat difficult to negotiate, you can thank the lunar low, which continues to have a bearing on your life today and tomorrow. For the moment, you need to continue your plans for the future, whilst at the same time avoiding making too many changes without taking time to ponder. A steady, family-motivated day will work best.

24 WEDNESDAY
Moon Age Day 7 Moon Sign Virgo

It is quite likely that you will find yourself at odds with someone today, most likely over issues that go back a long way. You remain essentially diplomatic in your approaches, but you don't have any control over the way others behave. All that is really necessary is that you keep your cool.

25 THURSDAY
Moon Age Day 8 Moon Sign Libra

It seems as though you are real lover of freedom at the moment and you would not take kindly to being held back. Whatever you know you can't do – that's what you wish to undertake. Pisces isn't usually awkward, but there is a slight tendency for you to be so under prevailing trends.

26 FRIDAY
Moon Age Day 9 Moon Sign Libra

Handling several different projects at the same time ought to be a piece of cake at this stage of the week. You plough into new projects with great enthusiasm and will co-operate with others marvellously. Not everything in the garden is lovely, though, because there could be some disputes at home.

27 SATURDAY
Moon Age Day 10 Moon Sign Scorpio

Great social encounters are on the cards and this could be a weekend to remember for some sons and daughters of Pisces. Remove yourself immediately from situations of confrontation, because they are not necessary or productive. Romance should begin to play a bigger part in your life this weekend.

28 SUNDAY
Moon Age Day 11 Moon Sign Scorpio

Family matters and the domestic scene generally are likely to be of most interest to you today, whether you work on a Sunday or not. Whatever you do today, you are likely to have one eye on your nearest and dearest and you could be worrying unnecessarily on their behalf.

29 MONDAY
Moon Age Day 12 Moon Sign Scorpio

With everything to play for, you need to put in maximum effort at the start of this week. As far as your work is concerned, you can make yourself into a real linchpin and will be putting in so much thought and effort that superiors could hardly fail to notice just how capable and organised you are.

30 TUESDAY
Moon Age Day 13 Moon Sign Sagittarius

What a great time this would be for the sort of simple pleasures in which Pisces revels. You don't need too much in order to be happy and it certainly isn't the material side of life that appeals to you too much at the moment. Good company, plain and simple food and feelings of contentment work best.

July

2015

YOUR MONTH AT A GLANCE

(+) = Opportunities are around   ⬤ = Be on the defensive   ⬤ = Life is pretty ordinary

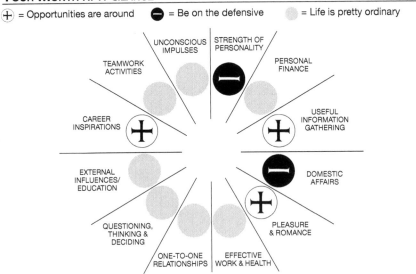

JULY HIGHS AND LOWS

Here I show you how the rhythms of the Moon will affect you this month. Like the tide, your energies and abilities will rise and fall with its pattern. When it is above the centre line, go for it, when it is below, you should be resting.

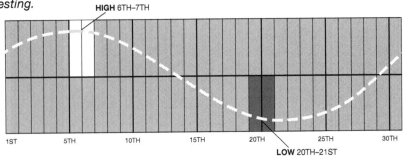

84

1 WEDNESDAY
Moon Age Day 14 Moon Sign Sagittarius

Today would be especially good for getting out and about with friends, even if most of the day is taken up with work. In what few spare moments you do have, ring the social changes and avoid going to the same old places. New incentives are knocking on the door of your inner mind, even if you don't exactly realise the fact.

2 THURSDAY
Moon Age Day 15 Moon Sign Capricorn

Business probably comes before pleasure today, but that won't be too much of a problem because you can mix and match both at present. Pisces is finding fun almost anywhere and your laughter is apt to be quite infectious. There are planetary positions around you now that simply make you happy to be alive.

3 FRIDAY
Moon Age Day 16 Moon Sign Capricorn

This would be one of the best days of the month for getting involved in new cultural projects, and a period for proving to yourself and the world how intellectual you really are. A few routine jobs will get left on the shelf, but if you are really lucky someone else will deal with them in any case.

4 SATURDAY
Moon Age Day 17 Moon Sign Aquarius

When it comes to expanding your horizons this could turn out to be a good time. You will have the opportunity to get rid of outmoded concepts and to look forward very positively. The only slight drawback today is that someone else tends to hold you back and probably for purely selfish reasons.

5 SUNDAY
Moon Age Day 18 Moon Sign Aquarius

It may be best to keep to tried and tested paths, at least for today. The inspirational Piscean comes along on Monday but for the moment you would be better off not pushing your luck or your physique too much. This almost certainly will not be an issue, because you are in the mood for relaxation.

6 MONDAY
Moon Age Day 19 Moon Sign Pisces

With everything to play for and the level of general luck probably better than it has been for a number of weeks, this is the time during July when you can make the world your oyster. It seems as if time is like elastic, because you have the ability to get so much done and friends should prove to be indispensable.

7 TUESDAY

Moon Age Day 20 Moon Sign Pisces

The positive trends should continue today, but will display themselves in a slightly different way. What you need now is to have a good time and in order to fulfil this desire you may be laying down some of the ordinary responsibilities of life. Find something to do that pleases you but that also stretches your capabilities.

8 WEDNESDAY

Moon Age Day 21 Moon Sign Aries

Whatever you are doing today, it will prove quite easy to bring a sense of harmony to life. A slower pace is likely, but it is one of your choosing and not something that is foisted upon you by circumstance. Understanding the way the world works seems to be child's play for you, even if it confuses your friends at the moment.

9 THURSDAY

Moon Age Day 22 Moon Sign Aries

Don't be afraid to take good ideas and to act on them, especially where your work is concerned. It is likely that you can simplify issues that others are making unnecessarily complicated and you won't do yourself any harm on the way. The right people are watching you at present and will like what they see.

10 FRIDAY

Moon Age Day 23 Moon Sign Taurus

You are at your most persuasive on this summer Friday and prove to be so charming that it is doubtful that anyone would deny you your way. With a tremendous sense of humour at present, you make everyone laugh and bring a breath of fresh air to just about any situation in which you are involved.

11 SATURDAY

Moon Age Day 24 Moon Sign Taurus

General progress is possible, no matter where you turn your mind at this time. Everyday routines could appear quite tedious and you operate best when you can ring the changes and when you are allowed to do things your own way. Keep in touch with friends right now and especially those at a distance.

12 SUNDAY

Moon Age Day 25 Moon Sign Taurus

Easier solutions appear out of the mist and once again you prove your ability to sort things out whilst your colleagues or friends are flapping around. In some ways this will increase your popularity, but don't expect everyone to be grateful. Just carry on in that calm and happy Piscean way.

13 MONDAY
Moon Age Day 26 Moon Sign Gemini

It looks as though you are on a perpetual quest for knowledge at the moment and you will not be content until you find an answer for almost everything. This is not typical behaviour for your zodiac sign and so you might surprise yourself, especially with your present tenacity. Try to relax later in the day.

14 TUESDAY
Moon Age Day 27 Moon Sign Gemini

Social relationships are likely to be looking especially good and it is towards a greater mixing and mingling with the world at large that you turn your attention this week. Finances are well starred today, so you might decide to splash out on something you have wanted for a while.

15 WEDNESDAY
Moon Age Day 28 Moon Sign Cancer

You are very incisive in your judgements and your comments go straight to the heart of most matters. This is a quality others lack and one or two people may be slightly envious of you at the moment. Don't react to provocation, but rather turn your attention towards people who are relaxed and happy.

16 THURSDAY
Moon Age Day 0 Moon Sign Cancer

This is a time during which you may begin to notice overall improvements to practical matters in the workplace and you are clearly working at your best. It is now the case that most of your really happy interludes are away from home and your mind is beginning to become more expansive generally.

17 FRIDAY
Moon Age Day 1 Moon Sign Leo

Plan now for the weekend, because today is best spent organising rather than doing. This would be an excellent time to be concentrating on the written word and even the most unlikely book can have some important advice for you. Take life lessons wherever you find them.

18 SATURDAY
Moon Age Day 2 Moon Sign Leo

There will be changes to your normal routines around this time, though most of them are likely to come about as a result of your intervention. What could annoy or upset you are those occasions when others insist they know better than you about how you should be living your life.

19 SUNDAY
Moon Age Day 3   Moon Sign Leo

Just at the moment you can be driven by emotional convictions and it is possible that some of your actions will look a little strange when seen from the perspective of others. If you realise this, you will also take the time out to explain yourself and so avoid any problems as a result.

20 MONDAY
Moon Age Day 4   Moon Sign Virgo

You want to see results from your efforts, but might have to realise that some of these are going to come a little further down the line. As long as you do not have too many great expectations this should be a settled and generally contented interval, but it certainly is not a time for pushing your luck.

21 TUESDAY
Moon Age Day 5   Moon Sign Virgo

Put your charm to the test at this stage of the week. Although the lunar low remains around for the first few hours of the day, it won't take long before you are feeling more cheerful and also more mischievous. Keep someone who is in a position of influence firmly on your side, because he or she will prove very useful.

22 WEDNESDAY
Moon Age Day 6   Moon Sign Libra

Matters at work could move ahead more swiftly now and you appear to have what it takes to be in greater control of your own destiny. If not everyone agrees with either your point of view or your strategy, you could try a little subterfuge in order to bring them round. If that fails, carry on anyway!

23 THURSDAY
Moon Age Day 7   Moon Sign Libra

You are in the midst of a period of mental and physical efficiency and tend to be very ordered in the way you do things. This is especially true today. If there is any problem at all, it will be because those around you have a different strategy and possibly one that will slightly annoy you.

24 FRIDAY
Moon Age Day 8   Moon Sign Libra

There is well-intentioned support coming from friends today, but you might feel you are being stifled. Don't turn down the advice on offer simply because you think you know better. Listen patiently and then decide for yourself in any case. Your patience is not up to scratch today, but it soon will be again.

25 SATURDAY
Moon Age Day 9 Moon Sign Scorpio

You enter a phase during which new ideas become a strong motivating factor. Pisces is sometimes inclined to stick to what it knows, but this is often because of a lack of personal confidence. It is hard to launch yourself into the unknown, but if you really want to progress this will be necessary during the next month or so.

26 SUNDAY
Moon Age Day 10 Moon Sign Scorpio

Your ego is boosted by the fact that almost everyone you meet seems to heap warmth upon you. Arguments are not likely at this time and you show just how diplomatic you can be. Is it the world that is treating you especially well or you who is showing greater optimism in life? In the end, it's the same thing.

27 MONDAY
Moon Age Day 11 Moon Sign Sagittarius

The new week brings a more impulsive phase and you need to be slightly careful that your enthusiasm doesn't run away with you. Keep a weather eye out for those who are trying to dupe you in some way and avoid signing any sort of document at the moment unless you have read the small print very carefully.

28 TUESDAY
Moon Age Day 12 Moon Sign Sagittarius

Whilst things are likely to go very well at work today, it might seem as though someone at home has a problem or two. Clear the air if you have the chance, because what you don't want right now is to leave issues to deteriorate. Routines might seem essential today, but you will find some of these very tedious.

29 WEDNESDAY
Moon Age Day 13 Moon Sign Capricorn

Choose carefully this Wednesday before you embark on any new adventure, because you could so easily be spoiled for choice. Whatever you decide to do it is important to give yourself to it one hundred percent. What you probably should not do today is to spend your time doing laborious tasks that will put you in a bad mood.

30 THURSDAY
Moon Age Day 14 Moon Sign Capricorn

Take the time to consider the feelings of those around you today. This is usually a quite natural process for you, but there is just a chance that you are slightly less responsive to the world at large than would normally be the case. Attitude is also important when dealing with situations that have a bearing on your working life.

31 FRIDAY
Moon Age Day 15 Moon Sign Aquarius

You could be feeling unusually sensitive at this time and would easily be upset by remarks that would have been like water off a duck's back a couple of days ago. Try not to react to such situations until you have had time to think about them, but also remember to get on with your life instead of fretting.

August

2015

Your Month at a Glance

⊕ = Opportunities are around   ⬤ = Be on the defensive   ◯ = Life is pretty ordinary

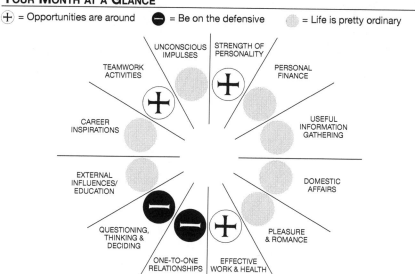

August Highs and Lows

Here I show you how the rhythms of the Moon will affect you this month. Like the tide, your energies and abilities will rise and fall with its pattern. When it is above the centre line, go for it, when it is below, you should be resting.

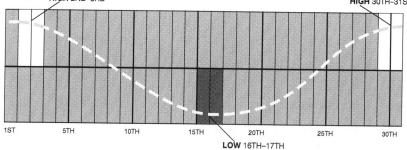

1 SATURDAY
Moon Age Day 16 Moon Sign Aquarius

It looks as though today the Moon acts as something of a brake – not in a physical sense, but with regard to the way you think. You sense that something really good lies just around the corner, but probably cannot see it for the moment. Patience is a virtue that Pisces has been given by Providence and now is the time to use it.

2 SUNDAY
Moon Age Day 17 Moon Sign Pisces

It could seem as if a coiled spring has been released today, because the lunar high allows all that pent-up energy to be released in an instant. A little faith and a good deal of optimism can go a long way and you really do need to believe in yourself if you want to get the very best out of today. Call on the assistance of friends.

3 MONDAY
Moon Age Day 18 Moon Sign Pisces

This could prove to be a real red-letter day and you won't want to waste a minute in your quest for personal success and – surprise, surprise! – personal glory. Even Pisces wants to be noticed sometimes and this proves to be the case under present trends. However, whether you will remain happy when in the limelight remains to be seen.

4 TUESDAY
Moon Age Day 19 Moon Sign Aries

Certain everyday discussions take on a slightly new feel now because it feels as though you suddenly have far more influence in certain directions. Use this wisely and try not to concentrate on too many matters at the same time. If you fail to use a little discretion you could end up in an unwanted argument.

5 WEDNESDAY
Moon Age Day 20 Moon Sign Aries

Finances are highlighted at the moment, so if they're not showing continued improvement it could be that you are not affording them the attention they rightfully deserve. You have some ingenious ideas at present and won't be at all reserved about sharing them with others, despite the fact that Pisces is sometimes inclined to hide its light somewhat.

6 THURSDAY
Moon Age Day 21 Moon Sign Aries

Getting along in any sort of relationship doesn't have to be a battle, something that you realise even if other don't. It's time to suppress the present tendency to defend yourself before you are attacked and to listen to what others are saying before you react. The more relaxed and easygoing Pisces should be well in evidence.

7 FRIDAY
Moon Age Day 22 Moon Sign Taurus

When it comes to getting ahead in a financial sense it is all down to good judgement, something that Pisces has in boatloads. Don't allow your decisions to be coloured by the opinions of others. Instead, do whatever is necessary to get things going smoothly on the cash flow front. This may require actions that are not universally liked.

8 SATURDAY
Moon Age Day 23 Moon Sign Taurus

Get ready to rush ahead if necessary, especially if you are at work today. You won't want to miss out on any opportunity that presents itself and can move at lightning speed when you know it is necessary. As busy as you are likely to be right now, you will still find the time to support less-motivated friends.

9 SUNDAY
Moon Age Day 24 Moon Sign Gemini

Your social life is likely to be on a roll and this will bring emotionally uplifting experiences when they seem to matter the most. Although you seem very cool to others, Pisces is often quaking a little inside. This is especially the case when you are put into the public eye. However, you are super-confident right now.

10 MONDAY
Moon Age Day 25 Moon Sign Gemini

Everyday matters should be both interesting and informative at the moment, and you will embark on new projects with a great deal of confidence and a determination to succeed. Not everyone around you is going to share your present optimism, and if you have any task at all today it will be cheering up those who are down in the dumps.

11 TUESDAY
Moon Age Day 26 Moon Sign Cancer

Ingenuity will be the key to success as far as money is concerned, maybe because you can somehow make a silk purse out of a sow's ear. Whatever you do, you need to remain positive about the outcome of enterprises and should not be deterred by the fact that there are one or two deeply pessimistic types around just now.

12 WEDNESDAY
Moon Age Day 27 Moon Sign Cancer

Your ego is likely to take charge today and as a result you won't take kindly to people trying to correct you. This trend has more of a practical than a personal application, so your love life and relationships in general remain unaffected. Nevertheless, you are more easily upset than might normally be the case.

13 THURSDAY
Moon Age Day 28 Moon Sign Leo

Meetings with new individuals could prove to be quite pleasant and you are certainly going to be opening yourself up to some unique situations. You are curious about more or less everything, and it is evident that you relish testing yourself in a number of different ways. Friendships prove to be extremely important now.

14 FRIDAY
Moon Age Day 29 Moon Sign Leo

You benefit at the moment from a diversity of interests, which is one of the reasons why you would enjoy a holiday so much under prevailing trends. That might not be possible, but you can ring the changes no matter what your present circumstances. Even small alterations to your routines would seem like a sort of vacation.

15 SATURDAY
Moon Age Day 0 Moon Sign Leo

This can be a great August day for you and should prove to be a marvellous time to be around the people you love the most. Make this a very special day by showing how much you care. People are used to Pisces being affectionate, but the difference today is that you can find the time to prove the fact in a concrete way.

16 SUNDAY
Moon Age Day 1 Moon Sign Virgo

It might be quite difficult today to get an objective picture of yourself or your actions and as a result you could easily take inappropriate actions. Better to do nothing at all than to march forward into situations that are only going to bring you problems later. Spend some time at home with family members and relish the chance of a break.

17 MONDAY
Moon Age Day 2 Moon Sign Virgo

Once again it would be better to put some plans on hold, rather than to get everything wrong simply because you don't have what it takes to follow through. The lunar low will be gone after today and there isn't much point in trying to swim against the prevailing tide. You should find plenty to do that is not remotely contentious.

18 TUESDAY
Moon Age Day 3 Moon Sign Libra

Deeper and more profound emotions tend to surface for a few days, but there is nothing particularly unusual about that in the case of your zodiac sign. What it does mean is that you will be more easily bruised and that you won't necessarily be giving all your attention to the more practical aspects of life.

19 WEDNESDAY *Moon Age Day 4 Moon Sign Libra*

A boost to personal relationships means that you can expect significant rewards from your partner or sweetheart. Out in the wider world, be careful not to react to everything you hear, because it's possible that some people are simply not telling the truth. As a result you might feel slightly stupid later.

20 THURSDAY *Moon Age Day 5 Moon Sign Libra*

Though your level of self-confidence is certainly not low, there are occasions around now when you will feel your nature to be eclipsed by that of more powerful and dynamic types. Though understandable, this is not really an issue. You get where you want to be in life, even if you don't make too much noise about it.

21 FRIDAY *Moon Age Day 6 Moon Sign Scorpio*

You are likely to be at the front of the queue when it comes to speaking your mind today. This is fine, just as long as your remarks are considered and kind. What you need to avoid is shooting too much from the hip. It would now be quite easy to give offence without intending to do so.

22 SATURDAY *Moon Age Day 7 Moon Sign Scorpio*

The weekend is all about mixing – and on a number of different fronts. Travel looks good and would be certain to broaden your mind. Whether or not you can get those around you to be quite as motivated as you are is open to doubt, but you are more than likely to have a go. Optimism is ever present now.

23 SUNDAY *Moon Age Day 8 Moon Sign Sagittarius*

This would seem to be a very good time to express your feelings and it is likely that the arrival of Sunday will give you the opportunity to do so. Family gatherings are a definite possibility and you might even be seeing people who don't come into your life directly very often.

24 MONDAY *Moon Age Day 9 Moon Sign Sagittarius*

This may well prove to be a good time for problem-solving. Your mind is very analytical and when others get stumped by details you see clear to the heart of many matters. Attitude is very important when dealing with people who are clearly too sensitive for their own good.

25 TUESDAY
Moon Age Day 10 Moon Sign Sagittarius

The Sun has now moved out of your solar eighth house and as a result you begin to feel far less restless and more willing to accept situations the way they are. A sort of satisfaction is likely to descend and today offers new opportunities for advancement, some of which are likely to come like a bolt from the blue.

26 WEDNESDAY
Moon Age Day 11 Moon Sign Capricorn

A lengthy discussion could help you to solve a problem that has been on your mind for quite some time. Friends should seem to be very approachable, but the real fact is that you are more willing to spill the beans. Pisces can sometimes be very closed and insular, but this is not the case right now.

27 THURSDAY
Moon Age Day 12 Moon Sign Capricorn

Routines today should seem fairly comfortable and you are jogging along, rather than breaking into any sort of run. What you might choose to do is to get yourself ready for far more hectic times to come. If there are any outstanding issues at work, you might decide to get these out of the way.

28 FRIDAY
Moon Age Day 13 Moon Sign Aquarius

It could feel as though you are going through a sort of transitional period, and this is brought about by the Moon as it passes through your solar twelfth house. This is a monthly event that is more significant to Pisces than any other zodiac sign, but at least it comes just before the lunar high.

29 SATURDAY
Moon Age Day 14 Moon Sign Aquarius

It is around this period that you may feel compelled to change your surroundings in some way. At the same time, you will wish to eliminate old situations that seem to have fulfilled all their objectives. Pisces is sometimes given to being restless and this is certainly the case close to the start of September.

30 SUNDAY
Moon Age Day 15 Moon Sign Pisces

Energy levels are now likely to be high and the next two days could mark the luckiest period for a few weeks. This would be an ideal time for travel, so much the better if you have decided to leave your holidays until now. You revel in good company and the chance to speak your mind.

31 MONDAY
Moon Age Day 16   Moon Sign Pisces

You need to commit yourself to new opportunities as and when they arise. Don't be too quick to speak your mind today, because it would be quite easy to say too much. Routines are likely to seem very boring and you will do almost anything to get out of jobs you see as being either tedious or distasteful.

September
2015

(+) = Opportunities are around　　● = Be on the defensive　　● = Life is pretty ordinary

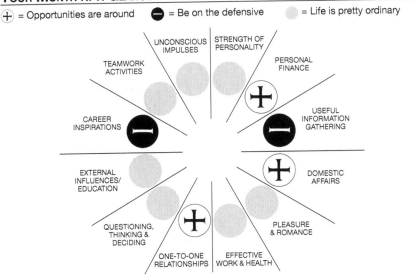

UNCONSCIOUS IMPULSES

STRENGTH OF PERSONALITY

TEAMWORK ACTIVITIES

PERSONAL FINANCE

CAREER INSPIRATIONS

USEFUL INFORMATION GATHERING

EXTERNAL INFLUENCES/ EDUCATION

DOMESTIC AFFAIRS

QUESTIONING, THINKING & DECIDING

PLEASURE & ROMANCE

ONE-TO-ONE RELATIONSHIPS

EFFECTIVE WORK & HEALTH

SEPTEMBER HIGHS AND LOWS

Here I show you how the rhythms of the Moon will affect you this month. Like the tide, your energies and abilities will rise and fall with its pattern. When it is above the centre line, go for it, when it is below, you should be resting.

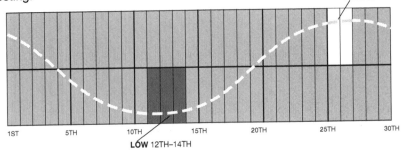

HIGH 26TH–27TH

1ST　　5TH　　10TH　　15TH　　20TH　　25TH　　30TH

LOW 12TH–14TH

1 TUESDAY
Moon Age Day 17 Moon Sign Aries

Intimate relationships look especially good at present, at least partly because you sense and understand the feelings of others particularly well. You need to broaden your mind at every possible opportunity right now and might be in the market for a journey or two that hadn't been planned earlier.

2 WEDNESDAY
Moon Age Day 18 Moon Sign Aries

Your sense of security and peace of mind is boosted by present planetary trends and although you may show the quieter side of your nature on occasions today, in the main life should be running fairly smoothly. Don't be too quick to crawl into your shell in the evening, just because you feel slightly threatened.

3 THURSDAY
Moon Age Day 19 Moon Sign Taurus

Uncharacteristically you might mishandle a personal encounter today. This could be because you are simply too busy to pay attention, but is also a response to the present position of the planet Mars in your solar chart. Some extra care is necessary when dealing with a person who is definitely far too sensitive.

4 FRIDAY
Moon Age Day 20 Moon Sign Taurus

The main sources of joy and pleasure coming into your life at the moment are friends and colleagues. People generally are likely to be very entertaining and offer significant diversions from the mundane aspects of life. Social impulses are also good and you will actively want to mix as much as possible.

5 SATURDAY
Moon Age Day 21 Moon Sign Gemini

As far as your list of priorities is concerned right now, it looks as though you are giving a great deal of your time and attention to purely practical matters. This might leave less available space to concentrate on either social matters or personal attachments. Make a mental note to put this right later.

6 SUNDAY
Moon Age Day 22 Moon Sign Gemini

It might be best for the moment to suspend any major decision-making not because you are likely to make any mistakes, but simply because you are so busy dealing with matters that crop up more or less instantly. Pisces is quite energetic, so it should not be difficult dealing with physical tasks.

7 MONDAY
Moon Age Day 23 Moon Sign Cancer

Keep on the move at the start of this working week and show those who count that you have what it takes to go solo in certain tasks. You are witty and even quite sharp when you are away from work, which gets you noticed. Romance is likely to be on the cards for the week ahead, so plan something special today.

8 TUESDAY
Moon Age Day 24 Moon Sign Cancer

This ought to be a productive day and one during which you are willing to make almost any change you see as necessary in order to get where you want to be in the near future. In terms of communication, you show yourself to be very direct and far more willing than usual to push your luck generally.

9 WEDNESDAY
Moon Age Day 25 Moon Sign Cancer

Personal and professional aims become very achievable under present trends, and if you are working today you can make great use of what the planets are offering. Even if you are not committed to work, you will doubtless find constructive things to do that contribute to your life.

10 THURSDAY
Moon Age Day 26 Moon Sign Leo

What happens now depends almost entirely on the way you approach situations. All too often, you leave the decision making to others and simply tag along for the ride. If you can stay out in front and make the running yourself, adventure and excitement await. You are likely to be very direct in conversation.

11 FRIDAY
Moon Age Day 27 Moon Sign Leo

Both personal and professional aims seem to be easily achievable under present trends and you should also be in a very cheerful frame of mind. Although gambling is never to be recommended, it is true that your level of general good luck is higher than usual at the moment. Confidence to say and do the right thing is not lacking.

12 SATURDAY
Moon Age Day 28 Moon Sign Virgo

This is likely to be a much quieter day. Since the lunar low is preventing you from making the sort of progress you were starting to take for granted, you might have to work that much harder to gain your objectives. If matters can be left alone for a couple of days, you might be well advised to put them aside.

13 SUNDAY
Moon Age Day 0   Moon Sign Virgo

Don't push too hard, because you won't get what you want and will only exhaust yourself trying to do so. Rather, you should be clearing the decks for actions that come later, whilst also getting some rest and relaxation. Learning to read the stars and the way they guide you is easier for Pisces than for most.

14 MONDAY
Moon Age Day 1   Moon Sign Virgo

You get an insight into the day-to-day problems experienced by people you know well and this allows you to get even further into their shoes than usual. Being of help to others is a great part of your makeup and this really shows now. You could discover that attitude at work is very important.

15 TUESDAY
Moon Age Day 2   Moon Sign Libra

It seems that you have tremendous mental energy today and you relish any sort of challenge that stretches your mind. At the same time, you could be more physically invigorated than has been the case for a while and show yourself willing to push the bounds of what you once thought was possible.

16 WEDNESDAY
Moon Age Day 3   Moon Sign Libra

A mixture of self-improvement together with a desire to delve into the workings of life is what can set today apart as far as you are concerned. You won't settle for normal explanations of things that mystify you. You have your Sherlock Holmes head on at the moment and will be searching for clues throughout most of the day.

17 THURSDAY
Moon Age Day 4   Moon Sign Scorpio

Most of the people with whom you come into contact today will seem to be doing everything they can to make you happy. Actually, this has more to do with your own attitude than their actions, but it's the result that counts. You are likely to consider your glass half full rather than half empty at the moment.

18 FRIDAY   ☿
Moon Age Day 5   Moon Sign Scorpio

You could come across as being slightly more caustic than you intend to be at end of this working week. Count to ten before you lose your temper, especially with a family member, and remember that the way others see life is different from your perspective. It's rare for Pisces to be unreasonable, but is possible at the moment.

19 SATURDAY ☿ *Moon Age Day 6 Moon Sign Scorpio*

This may be a good time during which to say goodbye to certain aspects of the past that are no longer of any good to you. This process is by no means easy for many Pisces subjects, because they are inclined to hold on to things. If you have actually got to throw something away you might have to rely on a relative to help.

20 SUNDAY ☿ *Moon Age Day 7 Moon Sign Sagittarius*

If at all possible you should consider a change of scene today. This falls well in with the present trend you are going through and is necessary because it would be all too easy to feel slightly bored with life otherwise. Try to relax and if possible get yourself involved in meditation exercises, which are always good for Pisceans.

21 MONDAY ☿ *Moon Age Day 8 Moon Sign Sagittarius*

Your need to be the centre of attention could well be overwhelming at the moment and though this is quite unusual for Pisces, you actually gain something from being centre stage. Most of the things you do right now are geared towards getting yourself noticed and you might be quite miffed if you are ignored by anyone.

22 TUESDAY ☿ *Moon Age Day 9 Moon Sign Capricorn*

It is possible that you now find yourself in a position to drop everything in order to search for something more exciting. This trend has been with you for a few days and could be at its strongest today. It certainly would not do any harm to ring the changes or to find ways in which you can entertain others.

23 WEDNESDAY ☿ *Moon Age Day 10 Moon Sign Capricorn*

Around this time you could be aware that there are people or situations that no longer have any real part to play in your life. Getting rid of what is no longer either essential or even desirable would be best; but once again, such is the nature of Pisces that you will still find it hard to dump almost anything at all.

24 THURSDAY ☿ *Moon Age Day 11 Moon Sign Aquarius*

You are still socially prominent and will continue to be so until the far end of the weekend. With a great deal of energy at your disposal you can get through many jobs in a fraction of the time they would often take and you will also be able to steer others in a more sensible direction than the one they are presently choosing.

25 FRIDAY ☿ *Moon Age Day 12 Moon Sign Aquarius*

There ought to be no lack of confidence about you under present planetary trends and although you can still be quite restless in certain ways, you also have what it takes to settle to any task that you know is essential. You may concentrate much of your effort today on getting something sorted out at home.

26 SATURDAY ☿ *Moon Age Day 13 Moon Sign Pisces*

Now you are more likely to be out in front and leading the field. The lunar high gives you superior judgement and enough confidence to let those around you know you want to make the decisions. Routines are definitely for the birds today as you make up your mind instinctively and act very much on impulse.

27 SUNDAY ☿ *Moon Age Day 14 Moon Sign Pisces*

Many of your decisions appear to have lucky consequences at the moment. This is partly down to your actions, but is also a response to the lunar high. There is fluency in what you are doing and matters seem far more connected than might sometimes be the case. A great time to mix business and pleasure.

28 MONDAY ☿ *Moon Age Day 15 Moon Sign Aries*

Practical issues and your general daily routine look to be going fairly easily, but there could be some personal frustrations to be attended to at the moment. At this stage of the week you might have to rely on advice that comes from people you know are on your side. Friendship is very important now.

29 TUESDAY ☿ *Moon Age Day 16 Moon Sign Aries*

Your mind still works very quickly – so quick that it will be difficult for others to keep up with you. Stop and wait now and again, and allow friends and relatives to understand better how your mind is working. If you don't, there is a strong chance that disputes or even arguments could be the result.

30 WEDNESDAY ☿ *Moon Age Day 17 Moon Sign Taurus*

In spite of changes that seem to be happening around you, it looks as though you will be doing all you can to maintain the status quo. Think about the situation, because if this means you are stuck in some sort of rut, something should be done. Advice is on hand – but will you listen?

2015

YOUR MONTH AT A GLANCE

⊕ = Opportunities are around   ⊖ = Be on the defensive   ⬤ = Life is pretty ordinary

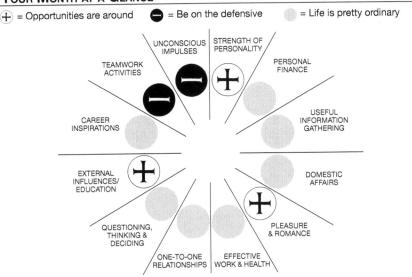

UNCONSCIOUS IMPULSES

STRENGTH OF PERSONALITY

TEAMWORK ACTIVITIES

PERSONAL FINANCE

CAREER INSPIRATIONS

USEFUL INFORMATION GATHERING

EXTERNAL INFLUENCES/ EDUCATION

DOMESTIC AFFAIRS

QUESTIONING, THINKING & DECIDING

PLEASURE & ROMANCE

ONE-TO-ONE RELATIONSHIPS

EFFECTIVE WORK & HEALTH

OCTOBER HIGHS AND LOWS

Here I show you how the rhythms of the Moon will affect you this month. Like the tide, your energies and abilities will rise and fall with its pattern. When it is above the centre line, go for it, when it is below, you should be resting.

HIGH 24TH–25TH

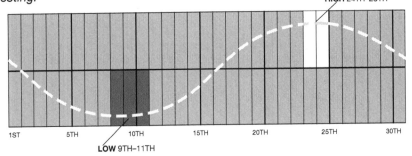

1ST   5TH   10TH   15TH   20TH   25TH   30TH

LOW 9TH–11TH

13 TUESDAY
Moon Age Day 0 Moon Sign Libra

Chances are that you will be focusing on the material side of life for today at least. If there is something you have been meaning to buy for your home, this could be as good a time as any to search it out. From a social point of view, you will probably be sticking to your inner circle around now.

14 WEDNESDAY
Moon Age Day 1 Moon Sign Scorpio

Once again it is towards possessions and the way you view them that your mind is apt to turn. You are entering a period during which 'things' will be far less important. It is for this reason that you continue to clear out your cupboards and drawers. It looks as though Pisces is deciding that it's best to travel light.

15 THURSDAY
Moon Age Day 2 Moon Sign Scorpio

Getting ahead of the game won't be difficult. It is on days such as this that you realise you are far cleverer than you sometimes appreciate and you need to turn your intelligence to your own advantage. Of course, you can help others on the way, but there are some people around who seem determined to stick fast.

16 FRIDAY
Moon Age Day 3 Moon Sign Scorpio

Both your popularity and your ego are likely to be extremely strong at the moment, and there is just a slight possibility that you are not taking the needs and wants of others into account. This is unusual for you, but is something that deserves extra attention.

17 SATURDAY
Moon Age Day 4 Moon Sign Sagittarius

Although there are significant challenges to be faced, you seem to be standing up to the pressure rather well. Pisces people are often shy and retiring, but this isn't at all the way you are likely to be coming across at the moment. There are signs that success could be on the way.

18 SUNDAY
Moon Age Day 5 Moon Sign Sagittarius

Don't expect everything to go your way right now, but when it matters the most you can pull out all the stops and show just how capable you are. Listen to what your friends say about you, because they know you are capable of almost anything. You may be surprised by some of the compliments that come your way today.

19 MONDAY
Moon Age Day 6 Moon Sign Capricorn

You might find that there are certain problems in the real world that need your attention almost immediately today. You are quite capable at the moment and will be inclined to see things from a very sensible point of view. If there is any problem at all, it will lie in getting others to follow your lead.

20 TUESDAY
Moon Age Day 7 Moon Sign Capricorn

If there is any chance at all to change your everyday routines right now, you should grab it with both hands. There is just a slight danger of boredom creeping in. Summer seems to have been a long time ago and Christmas, the next target for many Pisces people, is still a couple of months away. Give yourself a treat.

21 WEDNESDAY
Moon Age Day 8 Moon Sign Capricorn

The things that loved ones say at the moment are likely to have a lasting impact on you – which represents a very positive personal trend in an otherwise slightly sparse time. If you want anything much to happen today, you will have to put in that extra bit of effort yourself. This also means motivating others.

22 THURSDAY
Moon Age Day 9 Moon Sign Aquarius

Make the most of any professional opportunities that come your way, because you still might not be as content as you could be in your personal life. Get the dross out of the way and console yourself with the knowledge that the picture is slowly getting better.

23 FRIDAY
Moon Age Day 10 Moon Sign Aquarius

For the first time in a few days, your mind is like a dynamo today and with better trends opening up on all sides you have what it takes to make fireworks wherever you go. This is especially true in a romantic sense and you will be heaping on the compliments in a way that could sweep someone off their feet.

24 SATURDAY
Moon Age Day 11 Moon Sign Pisces

The Moon returns to your zodiac sign and since it will be working so well for you that has got to be good news. Take all your vitality today and aim it towards a dream that has been on your mind for quite some time. Even the impossible is not beyond the bounds of credibility. At the very least you could achieve a great compromise.

25 SUNDAY
Moon Age Day 12 Moon Sign Pisces

You continue to show a very positive face to the world at large. If you are seeking freedom, this is the time to make your pitch. In a physical sense, you are likely to be energetic and able to jump hurdles that would usually hold you back. Most important of all is your truly magnetic and attractive personality.

26 MONDAY
Moon Age Day 13 Moon Sign Aries

Communication is the present key to success. Talk, talk and more talk is the order of the day, and if you don't get involved in discussions at all levels you could lose out. Even when you have to deal with people you don't care for all that much, it is possible to achieve a consensus at the moment.

27 TUESDAY
Moon Age Day 14 Moon Sign Aries

This could be a very beneficial period when it comes to forward planning, but there are also some very strong social trends around. For these reasons, you could be carefully splitting your day between those matters that are of a practical nature and times when you simply intend to have a good time.

28 WEDNESDAY
Moon Age Day 15 Moon Sign Taurus

You are likely to be feeling good about yourself, but you might well display the fact in a fairly quiet way. Whilst others boast, you remain calm and simply get on with things. The knowledge that you know where you are going in life and how to get there can be quite satisfying.

29 THURSDAY
Moon Age Day 16 Moon Sign Taurus

Explore new ideas and go to open spaces. Your mind ranges far and wide under present trends and you need to feed it by looking at new possibilities. The end of October marks a time during which your curiosity is very easily aroused. If you are planning on taking a journey, make sure it's in good company.

30 FRIDAY
Moon Age Day 17 Moon Sign Gemini

All matters to do with home and family look fairly settled and with the weekend in view you may already be planning some sort of treat for those you love. For the moment, you are skipping along nicely, able to keep up the pace you have set for yourself and generally happy with life.

31 SATURDAY
Moon Age Day 18 Moon Sign Gemini

There is something of the pioneer about you as the weekend gets started. You won't be afraid to try new strategies and will respond well to changing circumstances. You show a real joy for life and this is hardly likely to be lost on the people with whom you live. During the weekend you could be looking hard at romantic possibilities.

November

2015

YOUR MONTH AT A GLANCE

⊕ = Opportunities are around   ⊖ = Be on the defensive   ◯ = Life is pretty ordinary

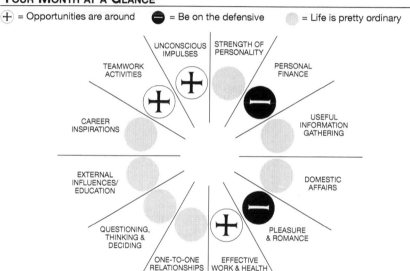

STRENGTH OF PERSONALITY

UNCONSCIOUS IMPULSES

TEAMWORK ACTIVITIES

PERSONAL FINANCE

CAREER INSPIRATIONS

USEFUL INFORMATION GATHERING

EXTERNAL INFLUENCES/ EDUCATION

DOMESTIC AFFAIRS

QUESTIONING, THINKING & DECIDING

PLEASURE & ROMANCE

ONE-TO-ONE RELATIONSHIPS

EFFECTIVE WORK & HEALTH

NOVEMBER HIGHS AND LOWS

Here I show you how the rhythms of the Moon will affect you this month. Like the tide, your energies and abilities will rise and fall with its pattern. When it is above the centre line, go for it, when it is below, you should be resting.

HIGH 20TH–21ST

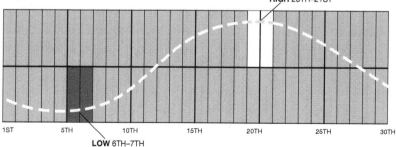

1ST   5TH   10TH   15TH   20TH   25TH   30TH

LOW 6TH–7TH

1 SUNDAY
Moon Age Day 19 Moon Sign Cancer

Where tasks have to be dealt with today it is clear that you want to do things your own way. You can even be a little cranky if things don't go as you wish and others will have to be careful not to step on your toes. What you can be sure of is that you will get most jobs done right first time.

2 MONDAY
Moon Age Day 20 Moon Sign Cancer

It looks as though Pisces is something of an explorer now and it is clear that you want to know what makes things tick. This might not be the best part of the year to take a journey, but any opportunity you have to break the bounds of the normal and to see new places should be grabbed with both hands.

3 TUESDAY
Moon Age Day 21 Moon Sign Leo

If you have to approach others today in order to gain the assistance you need to do things that seem important, don't forget to show your gratitude. Pisces can be just slightly offhand right now and that could lead to a little resentment. You will have the confidence to broach a difficult subject.

4 WEDNESDAY
Moon Age Day 22 Moon Sign Leo

Your intuition is stimulated today by any number of situations and you instinctively know when something looks or feels right. Don't be too quick to take offence at those who are genuinely doing their best and try to be as fair with the world as Pisces usually manages to be.

5 THURSDAY
Moon Age Day 23 Moon Sign Leo

Friendships can be great fun at this stage of the working week and you have every opportunity to make colleagues into pals. Trends show new people entering your life a good deal around now and at least one person looks like becoming someone who will be important to you for years to come.

6 FRIDAY
Moon Age Day 24 Moon Sign Virgo

With the lunar low coming along you will probably notice the pace of life slowing significantly. Your powers of discrimination are more limited and it will be easy to run out of energy. This is not an ideal day to embark on any new project that takes stamina and self-belief.

7 SATURDAY
Moon Age Day 25   Moon Sign Virgo

It appears that you have a very short fuse for the moment and you will probably have to count to ten in your dealings with people who tend to annoy you at the best of times. If you can't rely on the world at large, it looks as though you will have to fall back on your own resources. Pisces is now much quieter than of late.

8 SUNDAY
Moon Age Day 26   Moon Sign Libra

You are now entering a more emotional period and a time during which you are willing to talk about the deepest of issues. The inner workings of the Piscean mind are a closed book, sometimes even to you, but it looks as though you are now able to share these unexplored regions with someone else.

9 MONDAY
Moon Age Day 27   Moon Sign Libra

This is probably the best day of the month to be with loved ones and although the everyday responsibilities of your life are still present, it is those intimate moments that count for the most. Don't worry if you have a tendency to be reflective and quiet. The most important people in your life understand you very well.

10 TUESDAY
Moon Age Day 28   Moon Sign Libra

You may well prefer time spent away from emotional demands today and will have a light and airy approach to life generally. There probably won't be time for too much reflection or introspection in any case and the thought of having to untangle someone else's personal mess won't be too appealing.

11 WEDNESDAY
Moon Age Day 29   Moon Sign Scorpio

What a good day this would be for discussions and debates. Your wit is razor sharp and you will be able to make just about anyone laugh, which is halfway to gaining your objective. You could even be somewhat calculating in your approach at the moment; but if everyone wins in the end, does it matter?

12 THURSDAY
Moon Age Day 0   Moon Sign Scorpio

This is a great time to be with the ones you care about the most, whether you are doing something practical or simply having fun. You should be able to find something to do that stimulates your intellect, whilst at the same time proving to be quite educational. Trends show you are likely to forge new long-term interests now.

13 FRIDAY
Moon Age Day 1 Moon Sign Sagittarius

Concentrate on a specific issue today and don't get too carried away with the insignificant details of life that don't really count for anything. Friendships prove to be very important and new casual attachments seem to be forming for some of you. Getting really close to someone could be a different matter and might prove difficult.

14 SATURDAY
Moon Age Day 2 Moon Sign Sagittarius

With a slight change of emphasis in terms of planetary influences, it is now much easier for others to misunderstand what you are both saying and doing. Take just a little time out to explain yourself, because this can make all the difference. If you were looking for a peaceful and steady Saturday you could be somewhat disappointed.

15 SUNDAY
Moon Age Day 3 Moon Sign Sagittarius

As an antidote to yesterday, twosomes are well highlighted under today's trends and this would be the best part of the week to cement relationships that are important to you. Pisces doesn't want to go it alone and although you will still be quite happy with your own company, in the main you are content to have others on board.

16 MONDAY
Moon Age Day 4 Moon Sign Capricorn

Superiors are likely to be well disposed towards you this week, so you may as well ask for something you have been wanting for a while. This could be more than a simple pay rise and might have something to do with your ambitions for the future. Working in partnerships would be good under present trends, but finances are slightly variable.

17 TUESDAY
Moon Age Day 5 Moon Sign Capricorn

You should be quite happy to take ordinary, everyday responsibilities in your stride at present. You have the power to make your life more refined, cultured and comfortable, and you won't take kindly today to anything you see as being sordid or unsavoury. There is a greater sense of tidiness about you this week.

18 WEDNESDAY
Moon Age Day 6 Moon Sign Aquarius

A break from busy routines would clearly do you the world of good today; but do you have sufficient time to please yourself? It comes down to deciding for yourself, because nobody is forcing you to work so hard. Simply drop the reins for a while and let someone else do some of the driving.

19 THURSDAY
Moon Age Day 7 Moon Sign Aquarius

Organise your personal schedule well or you could run into some difficulties today, mainly born out of untidiness or rushing too much. One area of your life that looks extremely settled and happy is romance. There are words of affection passing back and forth today and a few of them could be unexpected.

20 FRIDAY
Moon Age Day 8 Moon Sign Pisces

You will now be putting new plans into operation and show every intention of breaking down barriers that have existed in a specific area of your life for some time. You are like an irrepressible battering ram, and you won't stop until you have achieved your objectives. This is the power of the lunar high.

21 SATURDAY
Moon Age Day 9 Moon Sign Pisces

You can make great gains by doing a host of new things today. Don't wait to be asked or you will lose the power of the moment. Now is the right time to ask for what you want – and maybe to take it in any case, if those around you refuse to listen.

22 SUNDAY
Moon Age Day 10 Moon Sign Aries

Make the right choices today and you could satisfy your desire to get together with other people. It's late in the year, but some Piscean people will now feel the pull of places far from home and a late holiday in the case of some certainly can't be ruled out. Even a short trip would make you feel happier.

23 MONDAY
Moon Age Day 11 Moon Sign Aries

Today is a good time to pursue more independent interests. You can't live other people's lives for them and right now you shouldn't even try to do so. New ideas pop into your head all the time at the moment and you show a tendency to turn these to your advantage. Just about anything you really want can be yours, with effort.

24 TUESDAY
Moon Age Day 12 Moon Sign Taurus

Fulfilment with your work now comes from the recognition you get from others. Colleagues and superiors alike should be telling you how talented you are and for once you might believe what they are saying. Keep a sense of proportion regarding a family argument that isn't half as important as it might at first seem.

25 WEDNESDAY
Moon Age Day 13   Moon Sign Taurus

Effort brings its own rewards today and what you end up receiving is definitely directly related to how hard you are willing to work. Standard responses might not work very well when you are dealing with your love life, and a little originality seems to be called for. That's not difficult for you, because you are as unique as they come.

26 THURSDAY
Moon Age Day 14   Moon Sign Gemini

Think ahead and plan for the future, whilst being willing to accept a slower and steadier way of going on than might appeal right now. No sooner are the difficulties of today apparent than they begin to disappear again. Stick to your guns if you think you are right about something, but don't argue about things more than you must.

27 FRIDAY
Moon Age Day 15   Moon Sign Gemini

There could be some fairly unusual opportunities to make new friends and to get together with the sort of people who are going to be very inspirational to you in the not-too-distant future. Gains come from the written word and from communications that come via technology, so keep an eye out for emails and text messages.

28 SATURDAY
Moon Age Day 16   Moon Sign Cancer

You seem to have all the drive and energy you could possibly need today, but that won't get you everything you want. Sometimes a little intuition is worth any amount of practical talent, and you are at your best now when it comes to seeing through others. You radiate confidence and that proves to be important.

29 SUNDAY
Moon Age Day 17   Moon Sign Cancer

Happy social encounters are possible and it looks as though you are coming to the end of something that has been a slight trial to you for a while now. This should leave your horizons uncluttered, and you are moving into a period when it would be sensible to spend a little time thinking about what you intend to do next.

30 MONDAY
Moon Age Day 18   Moon Sign Cancer

A bit of a gamble can pay handsome dividends, but only you and your intuition know when you should act. Expect positive results from your social and personal efforts and be willing to stick your neck out in order to get something you have wanted for ages. You are unlikely to venture too far today, because caring friends will hold you back.

December

2015

YOUR MONTH AT A GLANCE

⊕ = Opportunities are around   ⊖ = Be on the defensive   ⬤ = Life is pretty ordinary

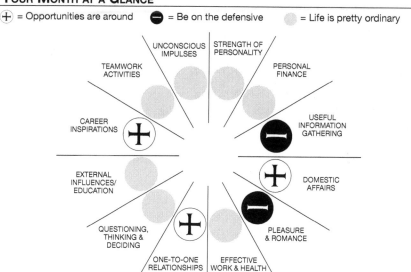

- UNCONSCIOUS IMPULSES
- STRENGTH OF PERSONALITY
- TEAMWORK ACTIVITIES
- PERSONAL FINANCE
- CAREER INSPIRATIONS
- USEFUL INFORMATION GATHERING
- EXTERNAL INFLUENCES/ EDUCATION
- DOMESTIC AFFAIRS
- QUESTIONING, THINKING & DECIDING
- PLEASURE & ROMANCE
- ONE-TO-ONE RELATIONSHIPS
- EFFECTIVE WORK & HEALTH

DECEMBER HIGHS AND LOWS

Here I show you how the rhythms of the Moon will affect you this month. Like the tide, your energies and abilities will rise and fall with its pattern. When it is above the centre line, go for it, when it is below, you should be resting.

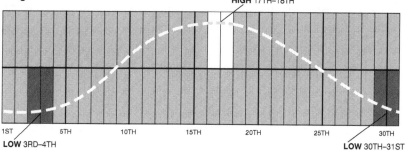

HIGH 17TH–18TH

1ST   5TH   10TH   15TH   20TH   25TH   30TH

LOW 3RD–4TH

LOW 30TH–31ST

117

I TUESDAY
Moon Age Day 19 Moon Sign Leo

It seems as if everyone wants to be generous to you at the moment and you would do well to accept the kind offers that are cropping up all the time. What people are doing is trying to repay you for the many kindnesses you have shown to them and this comes as proof of the sort of person you are.

2 WEDNESDAY
Moon Age Day 20 Moon Sign Leo

There is a tendency now towards greater intimacy, even with people who have been slightly distant in the past. Nevertheless, you remain generally adventurous and would be pleased to try something that might have seemed intimidating in the past. By this evening you could be organising social events for later in the month.

3 THURSDAY
Moon Age Day 21 Moon Sign Virgo

This will probably be a time of detachment and a two-day period during which you are not really connected to the world at large in the way you have been over the last few days. Treat this as a period for rest and relaxation and be willing to allow your friends to take some of the necessary strain.

4 FRIDAY
Moon Age Day 22 Moon Sign Virgo

Group situations prove to be especially rewarding, even if you tend to take something of a back seat for the moment. Although you sometimes use the period of the lunar low in order to retreat into yourself, this is much less likely to be the case today. On the contrary, you will feel the need of company.

5 SATURDAY
Moon Age Day 23 Moon Sign Libra

You have a good instinctive understanding of people's motivation today and will not be easily fooled by anyone who has the clear intention of misleading you in some way. What could really annoy you is jargon and red tape, because your penetrating mind wants to go straight to the heart of any matter.

6 SUNDAY
Moon Age Day 24 Moon Sign Libra

If you really want to get on today you will have to put in a good deal more effort than might sometimes be the case. On the other hand, you should probably ask yourself if this might not be an ideal day to relax a little and to enjoy the entertainment that is brought to life by the antics of family members and friends.

7 MONDAY
Moon Age Day 25 Moon Sign Libra

This may well turn out to be a day of hectic comings and goings. Keeping up with the general flow of life won't be at all easy, especially since the people around you seem to be doing everything they can to confuse matters. Rather than causing you irritation or distress, this situation should turn out to be funny.

8 TUESDAY
Moon Age Day 26 Moon Sign Scorpio

This may be the first real time during December that you have been able to give some time to thinking specifically about Christmas. Don't forget those all-important invitations and make sure that family gatherings are adequately organised. If there is one zodiac sign that needs to have the festive season sorted it's yours.

9 WEDNESDAY
Moon Age Day 27 Moon Sign Scorpio

Your desires now have a knack of turning out pretty much the way you might wish, even if you sometimes have to take a rather tortuous path in order to get things done. There is much humour about at the moment and you may well be in a more happy-go-lucky frame of mind than has been possible so far this month.

10 THURSDAY
Moon Age Day 28 Moon Sign Sagittarius

If there is a little more money around than you expected, hang on to it. With Christmas in view there is a danger you will be blowing everything you have on presents, but this could prove to be a mistake, not least because you may well discover some amazing bargains if you wait for just a day or two.

11 FRIDAY
Moon Age Day 0 Moon Sign Sagittarius

Your versatility is certainly on display at the moment and you will be tackling routine jobs in new ways. Although you have one eye on the upcoming festivities, you will also be very committed to the everyday requirements life has of you. There are some real advantages coming along in your personal life.

12 SATURDAY
Moon Age Day 1 Moon Sign Sagittarius

What probably matters more than anything today is concerned with keeping up an active and interesting social life. That shouldn't be too difficult at this time of year, but for the moment there are practicalities to be dealt with, too. Help a friend to find a solution to a long-standing problem.

13 SUNDAY
Moon Age Day 2 Moon Sign Capricorn

Career prospects have much going for them at the moment and you may find that you are taking on new responsibilities or else consolidating business gains you made earlier. At the same time, there are clearly going to be domestic issues that need your attention. All in all, this is likely to be a very busy day.

14 MONDAY
Moon Age Day 3 Moon Sign Capricorn

It is the material world that tends to attract your attention now. With everything to play for at the start of a new working week, you will want to be up early and getting on with a number of different jobs. This is just as well, because there are likely to be some notable delays coming for some of you.

15 TUESDAY
Moon Age Day 4 Moon Sign Aquarius

Your diplomatic skills turn out to be of particular importance now. When others fall out with each other, you find ways to play the honest broker. This is one of the most important gifts of Pisces and it allows you to get on well with everyone. As far as your own life is concerned, you should still be quite cheerful.

16 WEDNESDAY
Moon Age Day 5 Moon Sign Aquarius

This is not really the best time for new ideas. The Moon is now in your solar twelfth house and that is going to make you slightly more apprehensive and quieter than of late. What you do have right now is a tremendous ability to sort out the wheat from the chaff as far as new social contacts are concerned.

17 THURSDAY
Moon Age Day 6 Moon Sign Pisces

The green light is on and action becomes possible. Don't wait to be asked today, because it is very important for you to take the initiative. You respond well to the invitations that are coming in from other people and can easily handle about half a dozen different jobs at the same time.

18 FRIDAY
Moon Age Day 7 Moon Sign Pisces

With plenty of optimism and a self-belief that is far stronger than Pisces usually expects, you seem to be really motoring towards your objectives. Progress may only be slowed by the realisation that Christmas is just around the corner and some of your resources will have to be directed towards the celebrations.

19 SATURDAY
Moon Age Day 8 Moon Sign Aries

For those Pisceans who have recently been through slightly difficult times in a personal sense, attachments should now be easier to cope with. It may be that you can come to a new understanding or simply that your partner is now being far more reasonable. Put minor family worries to the back of your mind.

20 SUNDAY
Moon Age Day 9 Moon Sign Aries

Avoid being over aggressive regarding issues that would be best dealt with in a more diplomatic way. The trouble seems to be that you know very well how situations should be handled, but those around you have different ideas. You could be especially inquisitive today, maybe about a surprise gift.

21 MONDAY
Moon Age Day 10 Moon Sign Aries

Your love life is definitely favoured under present planetary trends. For those Pisceans who are between relationships, the run-up to Christmas could provide the embryo of something new and special. You might find a few frustrations developing at work, but you tend to take these in your stride.

22 TUESDAY
Moon Age Day 11 Moon Sign Taurus

This ought to be another fairly good day and one during which you are still keen to travel and maybe to visit people you don't see too often throughout the year. It is possible that personal attachments will be on your mind again, but now it is because love and romance seem to be offering so much.

23 WEDNESDAY
Moon Age Day 12 Moon Sign Taurus

Although you may seem to be slightly below par when it comes to communicating, in the main you will get on better today than you might have expected. See if you can get others to help you out with jobs that are irritating or boring. You respond positively to the little favours others afford you.

24 THURSDAY
Moon Age Day 13 Moon Sign Gemini

Christmas Eve brings good trends that help to make this one of the most positive and happy Christmas periods you have experienced for some time. Get the difficult jobs out of the way early in the day and, if possible, save some time to get to the shops. Most people hate town on a Christmas Eve, but not you. Look for some bargains.

25 FRIDAY
Moon Age Day 14 Moon Sign Gemini

You have so much going for you at the moment it will be difficult to know in which way to turn your attention. Not only do you have all the charm and humour that makes everyone else happy on this Christmas Day, but you should also be achieving a level of contentment that even Pisces rarely experiences.

26 SATURDAY
Moon Age Day 15 Moon Sign Cancer

You could turn out to be more compassionate and caring right now than is usual, even for your zodiac sign. Much of your attention will be heaped upon others and they tend to show their gratitude in a number of different ways. Some slight social embarrassment is possible if you say the wrong thing.

27 SUNDAY
Moon Age Day 16 Moon Sign Cancer

Today you are likely to be in a state of mind that looks inwards, rather than out towards the world in general, preferring family members to acquaintances or even friends. You might find excuses to stay at home in front of the fire. If you do push yourself, or are forced to do so because of prior arrangements, you might be pleasantly surprised.

28 MONDAY
Moon Age Day 17 Moon Sign Leo

In contrast with yesterday, this might be an ideal time to break with convention and to do something very different. You can take yourself and the world by surprise and will be extremely popular in the family if you suddenly announce that you want to do something really exciting. For the moment, you are avoiding routine like the plague.

29 TUESDAY
Moon Age Day 18 Moon Sign Leo

Now you show a generally positive face to the world and will be quite happy to take on more work, especially when you realise that extra effort now will mean more time to yourself later. When it comes to signing documents or taking on some new financial responsibility, make sure you have read the small print.

30 WEDNESDAY
Moon Age Day 19 Moon Sign Virgo

A chance word in the right direction could see you well set in terms of plans for the New Year. Despite the fact that you are fully enjoying what the festive season has to offer, it is also clear that you have one eye firmly placed on the future. In every respect, you can now keep more balls in the air than a juggler.

31 THURSDAY
Moon Age Day 20 Moon Sign Virgo

There are definitely helpful elements about on the path to progress today, even if some of them are disguised rather well. You tend to play the detective at present and will want to know how everything works. Stand by for some real surprises when it comes to tonight's celebrations.

How to Calculate Your Rising Sign

Most astrologers agree that, next to the Sun Sign, the most important influence on any person is the Rising Sign at the time of their birth. The Rising Sign represents the astrological sign that was rising over the eastern horizon when each and every one of us came into the world. It is sometimes also called the Ascendant.

Let us suppose, for example, that you were born with the Sun in the zodiac sign of Libra. This would bestow certain characteristics on you that are likely to be shared by all other Librans. However, a Libran with Aries Rising would show a very different attitude towards life, and of course relationships, than a Libran with Pisces Rising.

For these reasons, this book shows how your zodiac Rising Sign has a bearing on all the possible positions of the Sun at birth. Simply look through the Aries table opposite.

As long as you know your approximate time of birth the graph will show you how to discover your Rising Sign.

Look across the top of the graph of your zodiac sign to find your date of birth, and down the side for your birth time (I have used Greenwich Mean Time). Where they cross is your Rising Sign. Don't forget to subtract an hour (or two) if appropriate for Summer Time.

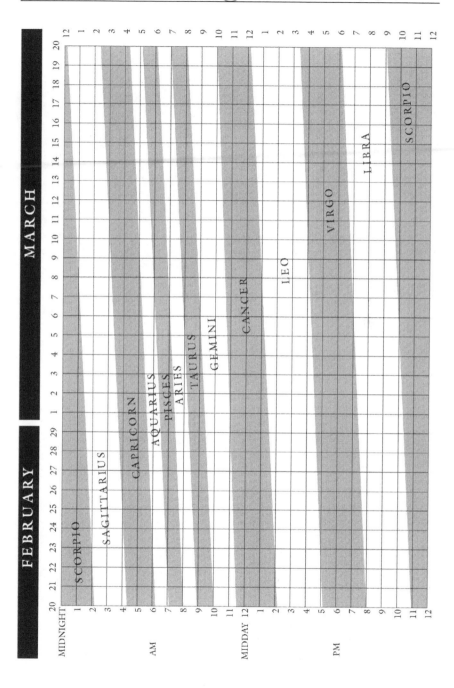

THE ZODIAC, PLANETS AND CORRESPONDENCES

The Earth revolves around the Sun once every calendar year, so when viewed from Earth the Sun appears in a different part of the sky as the year progresses. In astrology, these parts of the sky are divided into the signs of the zodiac and this means that the signs are organised in a circle. The circle begins with Aries and ends with Pisces.

Taking the zodiac sign as a starting point, astrologers then work with all the positions of planets, stars and many other factors to calculate horoscopes and birth charts and tell us what the stars have in store for us.

The table below shows the planets and Elements for each of the signs of the zodiac. Each sign belongs to one of the four Elements: Fire, Air, Earth or Water. Fire signs are creative and enthusiastic; Air signs are mentally active and thoughtful; Earth signs are constructive and practical; Water signs are emotional and have strong feelings.

It also shows the metals and gemstones associated with, or corresponding with, each sign. The correspondence is made when a metal or stone possesses properties that are held in common with a particular sign of the zodiac.

Finally, the table shows the opposite of each star sign – this is the opposite sign in the astrological circle.

Placed	Sign	Symbol	Element	Planet	Metal	Stone	Opposite
1	Aries	Ram	Fire	Mars	Iron	Bloodstone	Libra
2	Taurus	Bull	Earth	Venus	Copper	Sapphire	Scorpio
3	Gemini	Twins	Air	Mercury	Mercury	Tiger's Eye	Sagittarius
4	Cancer	Crab	Water	Moon	Silver	Pearl	Capricorn
5	Leo	Lion	Fire	Sun	Gold	Ruby	Aquarius
6	Virgo	Maiden	Earth	Mercury	Mercury	Sardonyx	Pisces
7	Libra	Scales	Air	Venus	Copper	Sapphire	Aries
8	Scorpio	Scorpion	Water	Pluto	Plutonium	Jasper	Taurus
9	Sagittarius	Archer	Fire	Jupiter	Tin	Topaz	Gemini
10	Capricorn	Goat	Earth	Saturn	Lead	Black Onyx	Cancer
11	Aquarius	Waterbearer	Air	Uranus	Uranium	Amethyst	Leo
12	Pisces	Fishes	Water	Neptune	Tin	Moonstone	Virgo

Made in the USA
Lexington, KY
15 March 2015